Praise for Ucal P. Finley's

DOG IN THE GARDEN

"Brilliant and poignant ….If you do not read another book this year, you need to read Dog in the Garden."
---- *Daryl L. McDuffie*
School Administrator, Author, Motivational Speaker

"…she captures the essence of dysfunctional mothers and how being a substance abuser affects their daughters."
---- *Gloria Finley*
Child Development Program, Marygrove College

From the Publisher

Dog in the Garden, based on a real-life story, is the first in a trilogy from award winning author Ucal Finley. The writer addresses two of the most prevalent issues that plague today's society, child sexual abuse and domestic violence.

In this first book, the narrator details five years of Gardena's harrowing childhood; living with an alcoholic, abusive mother, being sexually abused by her mother's lover and losing the protection of her two older brothers as they are sent to live with their grandparents.

DOG IN THE GARDEN

DOG IN THE GARDEN

UCAL P. FINLEY

Based on a True Life Tragedy of Innocence

This book is based on a true life tragedy of innocence. Names, places, dates and some incidents have been changed to protect the innocent.

Copyright © 2006 Ucal P. Finley
Cover Design: SOS Graphics and Printing

All rights reserved. No part of this book may be reproduced in any form or by any means, electronic or mechanical, including photocopying, recording, or by any information storage and retrieval system, without written permission from the publisher or author. This excludes a reviewer who may quote brief passages in a review.

Published by G Publishing, LLC
Detroit, Michigan

ISBN: 0-9788536-0-1

Printed in the United States of America

Library of Congress Control Number: 2006932012

DEDICATION

To God, who is the head of my life and who has blessed me with the gift of writing and continues to provide me with the strength to do so.

To my husband, who made sure he communicated with me while I was writing this book. Everyone knows that the key to a wonderful and long lasting marriage is communication; and he did an excellent job of discovering different ways to discuss our love, family, and this book.

My family and extended family are also in my gratitude. Without growing up with them, sharing in the times of happiness, despair and triumphs, this book would not be possible. Our experiences together brought the words on the following pages to life, thank you again.

To my mother and grandmother, who are constantly praying for me and asking God to "pour me out blessing that I will not have room enough to receive." He did when He blessed me with the two of you.

To my brother: I will always pray that God will ease your suffering and allow you to use the gift He has given you.

And to my children, Taz and Deuce', you are the best children in the world, and I am certain that one day your contributions to the world will be significant and long lasting. I love you.

ACKNOWLEDGMENTS

Thank you Ms. Julia Hunter, colleague and founder of G Publishing, LLC for your enthusiasm and encouragement. Because of you, I dusted off my manuscript and started writing again. Lydia Lacy and Erika Jones, thank you as well for the readings of my work that you have done and helping me decide on a title. Without the two of you, I would have probably published this work without a title that metaphorically captured the meaning as well as this one. And a special thanks to Ms. Stroud and Dr. Crisp. Both of you have been so instrumental and uplifting in all of my many discussed as well as completed endeavors. You are saints and will always hold a special place in my heart.

FOREWORD

The toll exacted upon individuals reared in a dysfunctional family is often measured by the success one attains in adulthood; however, a more revealing measure can be seen in the non-fulfillment of childhood dreams and aspirations. Broken dreams and the lack of parental guidance in assisting a normal child access to a quality education, thus enabling her to become more competitive in the workplace and subsequently a contributing member of society bemoan the indisputable responsibility concerning the role of caring and loving parents. The nurturing of young lives begins not at birth, but rather conception. Making and keeping regular appointments with the obstetrician, maintaining a regimen of a healthy diet and sustaining a stress-free lifestyle are key ingredients to producing a healthy child at birth. Once a child is born, the real work begins! For the next 18-23 years, the well being of the parent becomes secondary as the primary focus is and will be for an extended period of time, the overall nurturing of the child both physically and emotionally.

Ucal Finley has effectively provided the basic foundation concerning the consequences of ineffective child rearing. Benign neglect and false promises soon shatter the underutilized potential of an aspiring bright young woman. She ultimately begins to embark upon the path repeating the cycle with her own children if not for the loving concern of a grandparent, who, upon examining the errors of her child rearing experiences, decides to make a difference in the lives of others. It is that difference that eventually transcends the unacceptable notion that things and situations can't be reversed even under the worst set of circumstances. Although in the very best of financially secure families, making the right choices can often spell the difference in continued success or complete failure. Those without unlimited financial means are themselves subjected to the same decision making principles, only the end result can be much more catastrophic.

This book represents a broad vision of things as they are, things as they could be and certainly, things that should be. Ucal Finley has eloquently captured the breadth and essence of growing pains experienced under extraordinary circumstances along with the courage and determination to succeed at all cost.

--- Robert Crisp, PhD
Office of Fine Arts, Detroit Public Schools

DOG IN THE GARDEN

PROLOGUE

Woodward and Seven Mile was not the corner of choice for her, during her street walking days. It was however, one of the streets her pimp, Doug, required her to frequent. Long nights walking by the State Fair Grounds, kicking debris in the streets when traffic was slow and the night air hot; she leaned against street signs to rest her tired feet and to wave at potential Johns.

Every so often a male driver would creep up along the curb and ask, "You need a lift somewhere?" Her response, depending on how tired she was or brisk the night, could be a short, "Yeah." With her fumbling to quickly open the car door or "Sure daddy, it's the same place you going", which was her way of trying to be sweet enough to earn an extra tip for her services.

The street life took its toll on Lynn. Once a high school graduate, tall and thin. She was a beautiful promising young woman. She was never seen without having a perfectly made face or freshly pressed beautiful clothes. She was the promising one of five children. She was to be a secretary at a prominent company, a nurse, or school teacher. Instead she became a whore.

She met Doug not too long after high school and although she was a good girl, she was drawn to his badness. Doug had several lady friends, but that never bothered Lynn. Whenever she came around him, the other ladies knew that Lynn was special.

Lynn's mother warned her about Doug and men like him, "He's a pimp! And if that man have his way with you, you'll be sellin' yo' body to strange mens in the streets."

"Not true. He loves me." Lynn would always reply.

She had given birth to D-Man, the son of her pimp and things seemed to be going as she dreamed they would. Although she wasn't married to Doug, she believed the birth of her son would change that. It never did. As the rent went unpaid and the choices of shelter became scarce, it was time for Lynn to pull her weight.

"We need some money up in here girl." Doug spoke as he paced the floor convincing Lynn that she sat on a pot of gold. "Take that boy to yo' mama's to live for a little while until things get better."

"So we gonna get him back after a while, right?"

"Yeah. We'll get him back after we settle down

and then we'll have mo' babies. But for now I need you to do this for me–for us."
"But I don't know what to do or how to do it. It, it just don't seem right." Lynn was skeptical about what Doug was asking of her. She knew that prostitution was wrong. Her mind circled for another solution, but her job as a waitress didn't pay enough to sustain their lifestyle. And Doug's ability to control his other whores was slipping.
"Just do what you do with me baby. Pretend they me. Now I know you scared and all, I got something that'll take them fears away. It's gonna help you. C'mon." From the bedroom he led her down the hall to the dark, damp and musty bathroom that had gone unclean for months. She sat on the toilet and the smell of urine rose in the air from the toilet base. On the rusty sink bowl, stains of spat out toothpaste created a marble design, there was a used syringe, a spoon, a lighter and a white powder substance. "Hold out yo' arm." Taking his belt, he wrapped it around Lynn's thin arm. She never questioned him. She trusted him. As he mixed and heated the concoction, as she had seen him do for himself and the other women, she surrendered. "Now this might sting a little, but you'll feel good enough to do what you have to do for us." As the potion traveled through her veins, he loosened the tight belt from around her arm and it dropped to her side. She sat silently on the toilet. Lynn had never

been high before. She only took a sip of cheap wine every now and again, but this was no wine. This was heroin. Thoughts of what Lynn's mother said to her about Doug entered her mind. Visions of her youth in River Rouge played out like a small dramatic skit before her. She envisioned living in the tin roof two bedroom shack, sharing a bed with her younger sister. She remembered how neatly she kept her clothes and other things she was able to buy with her income from her job as a baby sitter. The neighbors loved Lynn. She was so dainty and delicate. She was always polite and trustworthy. Lynn would not play softball on the dirt roads with the other kids, she was too busy learning how to apply make-up. She didn't run in the fields catching fireflies with her sister, instead she would be catching the eyes of promising young men in the neighborhood. Lynn was a lady. And a lady would never lay down to make money. She would be respectable. A lady would work in an office, marry a good husband and have lots of children to make a home. As she drifted into numbness, forgetting all of those things she once dreamed of, Doug left the bathroom and with him left Lynn's dignity.

After years of walking the streets, using drugs, having another son fathered by a John, and being abused by Doug, Lynn found salvation in the arms of Richard. Richard was a white man she had met on the corner of Joy and American. He didn't pull up to the curb to have a good time, as Lynn asked, he saw a woman who needed help and he wanted to help her.

Richard refused to take her to the drug clinic to receive methadone treatments for her heroine addiction, he believed cold turkey and love was the only way to truly release her from her demon. When she ran to the toilet to vomit, he was there to rub her back and give her a shot of liquor. When she shook, had fevers and cold sweats, he spoke gently to her and gave her a glass of liquor. When her stomach cramped and muscles knotted, he gave her soup mixed with liquor. The long nights and days of her withdrawals were soothed by Richard and with liquor, until finally the spasms ceased. One vice was gone and Lynn felt as though she was a new woman. She was ready to greet the world once again in pressed clothes, a made face and the new baby she was carrying.

Richard took her to her prenatal care visits at the local clinic. He even took her the social services office in their neighborhood and helped her fill out the forms, in to receive her own income. But when Richard found out that the baby she was carrying was not his, he abandoned Lynn, but she was fine with that. She had a new place and a second chance. As she sat on her knees in the front yard of her home, planting a garden, weeks before the baby was born, she hoped and prayed for a little girl. Her daughter would be her own way of starting life over again.

The rose bush she planted months ago was already in bloom. The marigolds were arranged perfectly between the English ferns and the Elephant Ears. The Daylilies began to display their beautiful gold and orange colors.

"So Lynn, what are you gonna name that baby when it gets here?" A neighbor three doors down, walked over to ask her.

Lynn paused for a moment and placed her soiled garden gloves on her knees. Staring into her garden, softly she spoke the name, "Gardena".

"Gardena? Don't you mean Gardenia?"

"No." Lynn smiled as she slowly turned around to look at the woman. And with pride in her voice, as she turned back to scan over her garden she stated, "Gardena. She is gonna be as beautiful as my whole garden and as loved and pampered as each flower in it."

Chapter 1

LOVE NEGLECTED

Heartbreak was the beginning of it all. One after another with no end in sight, but fortunately for some, light does shine at the tunnel's end. The light might represent peace, joy and happiness, wealth or even death. The masses, however, are not so lucky. They continue to fall deeper and deeper into an abyss of sorrow. No hope is in view for them. No God, no glory or love is in store for the forgotten. It leaves them feeling abandoned. They are the children of the lost--bastard by a thousand fathers. Fathers who have mental illnesses, physical sicknesses, disease and torment. Unlike those who are just fathered, but without. Worse. Worse in that the life that is present becomes an undeniable reminder of the love that began and suddenly ended.

"Gardena? Gardena? Get yo' ass in here girl!"

"Yeah, Ma?" Gardena stood breathing heavily having run in from outside. She was a brown skinned short, thin child about six years of age with a full face and a round belly. Her hair was short and she sported four ponytails that stood in the air with barrettes hanging from the ends.

"This here's my baby girl." Her mother said while sitting in the kitchen talking to another male stranger.

He towered over her as he stood up to shake Gardena's hand. Unlike the other men who Gardena's mother claimed were all her uncles, this man could not be. This man was white. There was no way her mother could say he was related to them. Who was he anyway? Why was he in their home? These questions and more circled her mind as she stood still shaking his hand and studying his features. His hand felt hard and was hairy around the knuckles. The last man Gardena was introduced to was clean shaven, but this man had a long beard and mustache that had the appearance of never being groomed. His clothing read Jeremy and there was a Ford plant symbol over his right pocket. The blue coloring of his shirt now looked gray as though it had not been washed in months. The smell of his skin mixed with the oil reeking from his clothes left a musty sour aroma as he returned to his seat.

"Well? Say hi girl."

"Hi."

Gardena turned her head towards her mother, eyes full of questions that would go unanswered as usual. Her mother smiled at her and patted Gardena's head. Gardena loved her. She loved her mother as much as her mother loved the Po Pov she took to her lips every morning. She looked at her mother and thought she was the most beautiful woman in the world, but the reality of the mirror told a different story. Her story was full of pain, suffering and abuse. A story of a woman searching for fulfillment, yet settling for what life threw at her. She took a drag from her Pall Mall and gestured for Gardena to leave. Gardena turned and walked out of the front door.

She was alone with her mother this week as her brothers preferred to stay with their grandparents. Gardena had never met them, but she assumed they must be good people. Her brothers always wanted to go to their grandparents' home. Gardena's mother would say that they could as long as it was all right with their grandparents. The boys would run and pack their things and Gardena would hurry to pack hers as well. But her mother would never let her go over to her grandparents' house, nor did her grandparents ever come in to say hello to her when they picked up her brothers. One day, Gardena asked her mother why she could not go with her brothers. Her mother told her how her parents didn't want to be bothered with Gardena because she was so young. Gardena thought nothing of it since her mother spoiled her so much. However, Gardena began to notice a change in the family she had come to love. Her brothers began spending more time at their grandparents' home. Gardena's mother would spend days and nights yelling into the phone. Gardena had heard her mother tell the person on the other end of the phone, "You can't take my kids!" She heard screams from inside of the phone claiming her mother was a drunk. She had also heard the person say she would report her mother to the police. Her mother hung up. The phone rang again and again her mother hung up, until finally she took the phone off the hook. Gardena questioned her mother about the conversation and her mother's only reply was that the boys wanted to stay another week with their grandparents.

    Gardena couldn't fathom why her brothers didn't love Mama. Whatever they wanted Mama or one of their new uncles would buy. So why didn't they want to stay? They were just jealous she assumed. They knew like she did that Mama loved her best. This is why Mama spent so much time with her. Mama would comb her hair, press her clothes, and make her delicious pancake breakfasts every morning and these were all rewards for Gardena's dedication to her mother. They would never be loved by Mama the way Gardena was because they didn't love Mama.

CHAPTER 1 LOVE NEGLECTED

As the sun made its way far into the west and settled on the horizon of the earth, Gardena sat marveling at its beauty. It was peaceful living on Plainview Street. Not too many kids around to start trouble with their ugly ways, just a little girl, a few years older than Gardena, who she enjoyed playing with.

A car pulled into the driveway, as Gardena sat and thought of her pseudo-suburban life in the city of Detroit, and two men with two women got out of the car and headed towards the door. They were loud and laughing, using even more vulgar language than Gardena's mother had used. These were older looking men with very young looking women, maybe even younger than her mother. One of the men had his hand in the back of one of the women's pants, kissing on her neck as they approached the porch.

"Yo' mama here baby?" The woman asked grinning as the man continued to force one of his hands deeper into her pants, while beginning to rub on her breast with the other. Gardena stood in shock, somewhat afraid to answer the stranger. She had not seen such behavior from adults before. The lady switched the beer can she was holding into her other hand while fumbling with her cigarette.

"Wade," she laughed, talking to the man who was persistent with his groping of her. "Cut it out."

"Oh com' on baby, you wasn't saying that shit on

the way over here."

"Girl, did you hear me?" The serious heightened tone of the woman startled Gardena who instantly jumped and ran inside.

The white man who was sitting in the kitchen was now leaving from her mother's bedroom zipping his pants.

"What's going on Gardena?" he said as he began to button his shirt.

"There's some people at the door for Mama".

"Lynn? There's some people at the door for you." He said as he walked to the door to invite them in.

"Okay, I'm coming." Gardena heard her mother yell from the bedroom. Curiosity made her go to the door and peek through the crack, but fear kept her from pushing it open. She looked through the crack just enough to see her mother's tall naked body, as her feet were fishing for the sleeves of her pants leg. Gardena wondered what the man was doing in the room with her mother. Why the door was closed? Why was she naked? She hoped inside that he had not hurt her mother. Her mother was a god to her. Everything in life that she could be, everything and all she wanted to be. Her mother pulled the door open.

"Girl, what you doing standing by my door?" She pushed Gardena out of the way gently as she walked over to the strangers who were now in the house.

"Hey! How ya'll doin'?"

CHAPTER 1   LOVE NEGLECTED

"See you got the baby today." One of the women said.

"Yeah she just had to stay with me I was gonna send her to my mama's with the boys, but she didn't want to. I swear I can't breathe without that girl down my throat." Her mother spoke as though Gardena was in another part of the house.

"Really, girl I know how that can be."

"Yeah, so anyway what's going on? I got the drink, who got the smoke?"

They talked for what seemed like hours; laughing, drinking, toasting, smoking and moving their heads to the sound of music. They partied as Gardena stood looking from the kitchen. What did her mother mean by she couldn't breathe? It was hurting Gardena to think of what her mother had said. She was hurt that her mother was in pain because she chose to stay with her. No, she thought, her mother couldn't mean that. Her mother was playing around making jokes to entertain these people. These people Gardena felt should leave so that she and her mother could be left alone.

The talking continued as Gardena watched her mother walk into the kitchen and grab a fifth of Po Pov vodka from the shelf. She walked past Gardena without looking at her or even patting her head as she would so often do.

The man who was feeling on the woman outside

was now rolling what appeared to Gardena to be a cigarette. He licked and smelled it before putting it to his lips and lighting the slender roll of paper. He inhaled and coughed, saying, "Now that's good shit." He puffed it again before passing it to Gardena's mother.

One woman went over to the stereo and turned the music up loud. "Shame" played and the rhythm made her dance on her way back to her seat. The other woman stood to her feet dancing and gyrating her pelvis back and forth to the crowd of intoxicated on lookers. Her afro was full, light and shapely; and it moved with every motion of her body.

All Gardena wanted to do was join in, dance, sing, smoke and drink so that her mother could enjoy her presence as much as she did theirs. The laughing, the music and smoke, filled the air and became too much for Gardena to take. She wanted some of the attention that her mother was so freely giving the others.

"Ma?" The bass of the song was too loud for Gardena's soft voice to penetrate. "Ma?" *Mama just don't understand!* The lyrics of the music played in the fore ground of Gardena's attempts to get her mother's attention.

"Ma!" Gardena screamed and all heads turned with eyes fixed on her. The attention she wanted, but the wrong kind. The music still played loudly in the background, but no one danced or was singing along,

CHAPTER 1   LOVE NEGLECTED

instead, they all looked at Gardena, eyes locked. She was the person interrupting their freedom, their release, the break they needed from society, authority, religion and kids. The freedom life could only give with vodka and a joint. Yet there stood a shackle, beckoning them away from what life had robbed them of; the ability to live free.

"What?" Her mother shouted back in absolute disgust that she was there.

"I just wanted something to eat."

"Eat a sandwich. I'm busy." The crowd resumed their pleasurable activities of dancing, smoking, drinking, feeling and kissing as though Gardena was a news break that no one was interested in enough to continue listening to.

"I don't want a sandwich."

"Eat a hot dog then."

"I don't want that. You said you was gonna make some pork chops and..."

"Girl damn! I ain't got time for this shit. Eat what I said or don't eat nothing. Matter of fact, take yo' ass to bed. You don't want what I said, you don't eat nothing!"

"But ma..."

"Get yo' ass to bed girl. Now!"

Gardena ran to her room. No one stopped her mother to say please feed the child. Or to say her mother was wrong for not making her the dinner she had promised as Gardena thought they should. No. Everyone went back to their partying, their hate for others and love of themselves and Gardena entered her room and cried.

She sat still in the dark bedroom for fear of disturbing her mother again. All she wanted to remember were good times with her mother to take the pain away. She closed her eyes tight and pictured the night she, her mother and one of her uncles went to the Ford Theatre to see "Jaws". It was scary, but her mother held her during every frightening scene. Gardena felt warm thinking about the love her mother showed her that night, but as the night grew longer, the long caresses Gardena received became shorter and shorter until they were completely replaced with the cup her mother was holding. And although Gardena tried to push the image out of her mind, she couldn't help but remember the walk to the rest room with her mother.

"Ma, I gotta go."

"Okay baby, wait a minute." The intense look on Gardena's face was a state of urgency and this separated her mother from her drink.

"Alright, let's go." As they got out of the car, Gardena noticed the back of her mother's pants.

"Ma, the back of yo' pants is wet."

"Yeah, well, I couldn't make it."

The walk to the drive-in's restroom took forever.

CHAPTER 1 LOVE NEGLECTED

Gardena could hear people talk about the way her mother stumbled in the gravel and swagger as she walked. She heard a young boy loudly say, "Hey her wigs on crooked," and laugh with another kid. She heard a man say, "Damn, that bitch done pissed her pants!" and watched as others shunned away as they walked by. Never once did Gardena run away or let go of her mother's hand. She was hurt and embarrassed, but she wouldn't allow others to see it. This was her mother and she hated everyone for what they said and did to her. She was a beautiful person. Why didn't anyone else see this? She wanted all the people around to disappear and leave her mother be, but there was no magic to make this happen. So Gardena walked into the rest room with her mother, the drunk that couldn't be hidden.

It seemed as though Gardena had been in her room for hours and the more she thought about the times with her mother the more unhappy she became. But she was determined to be a better child for her mother. She knew in her heart that if she could prove to her mother that she loved her, her mother would stop the drinking, stop the smoking, stop having strangers in their home and give her love in return. All she wanted to live for was the love of her mother. Nothing else mattered.

There was nothing that could replace the warmth and special relationship she wanted with her mother.

She thought of different TV shows and how those mothers loved their daughter's and she wanted and needed that kind of relationship with her mother. She saw other mothers sitting on the porches reading with their daughters and she wanted that. She watched her friends talk with their mothers in loving ways without profanity and she needed that. There had to be a way Gardena could make her mother see she was special. She had to make her see she was as precious as her mother's weed and vodka, she was more valuable than strange men fixing their clothing as they left her mother's room. She was.

As she sat she thought of what she could do to make her mother see this. Gardena stopped crying and she began to make a list in her mind of what she could do. The loud music sometimes interrupted her thoughts, but she vowed to clean the house everyday, cook, at least cereal and sandwiches because she was too young to use the stove. And she would also make her mother a nightly bath and rub her feet afterwards with lots of Vaseline. This would make her mother see her love.

She closed her eyes and the music seemed to be drowned out by the darkness engulfing her, until there was only silence and she drifted to sleep.

Chapter 2

LONGING

Calm and peace through the surrounding sunlight could be felt throughout the room. Love renewed with the smell of fresh cut grass entered Gardena's nostrils as she struggled with the covers. Then fear set in. Where was her mother? Did she leave her in the house alone again? She fought hard to pull back the covers as they tried to paralyze her from arising. As she tried to awake, she felt something preventing her. The thing held her down laughing, keeping her from helping her mother. Her mother needed her now. Gardena had to find a way to overcome this demon, as it tried to destroy her will, her desire to find her mother. But the demon would not give in. It kept its restraints on her laughing as she began to cry, growing weaker with every move, until finally she sat up straight and screamed, "Mama!"

She looked around the room but no one was there. There were no strangers, demons, monsters or boogymen. Just Gardena in her small bedroom sitting among tangled covers, watching the specks of dust dance in the rays of sunlight.

"Mama?", she called again to the silence praying she was not left alone. If God could only help her overcome this fear, she would not feel so alone when her mama left her in the house by herself. "She must be in the bathroom", is what Gardena thought, but as she knocked on the door there was no answer. She turned the knob to see an empty bathroom and worried even more.

Slowly she approached the living room where the lusts of adult pleasures and self-gratification had taken place. She feared that her mama would be missing or even worse, hurt, unconscious or dead.

The hallway that led past the linen closet and towards the living room seemed longer than usual. Maybe it was anxiety that kept the hallway extending its length. The fright of seeing the inevitable demise of her fate----abandonment or destruction of her mother's being, made Gardena hesitant, but she continued moving on towards the living room. The house felt cold. The cold of a nursing home when the aide enters the room of a dead patient, still, clammy, spooky. This feeling engulfed Gardena and her heartbeats became faster and she could hear the pounding of her life. It got harder for her to breathe as though the oxygen was being vacuumed from the hallway and she felt faint. If only she could make it to the living room, she would pace herself quickly to the front door, turn the knob and be saved by the life giving beauty of God. She would breathe in slow, deep breaths of air, the power of the earth's nature, even in the city, would calm her beating heart. Then she would attend to the thoughts of her mother.

She turned right at the long stretch of hallway to find her mother on the floor with an empty half pint of Po Pov lying next to her. She froze with fear. No time to think of her own safety and well being she thought of before. She must attend to her mama. Without mama there was no Gardena.

She ran over to her mother's side, "Mama? Mama?" She shook her violently.

"What? What, gaddamnit?" Her mother turned from one side to another and fell back to sleep.

Gardena was relieved. Her mother was just sleeping. She didn't want to disturb this, causing her mother to fall out of love with her. So she left her side and decided to honor her promise of being the best daughter in the world.

She walked to the kitchen and opened the refrigerator. The refrigerator engulfed her in a chilled burst of air and she peeked through the smoky freon, searching for the milk. The refrigerator was full of goodies she and her mother bought the day before. The fresh fruit, oranges, pears and Granny Smith's apples that laid in the fresh crisper were Gardena's favorites. She moved the jug of Pure Fresh orange juice and the chocolate milk and grabbed the half-gallon of two percent milk. She knew her mother preferred two percent milk to whole milk. After placing the milk on the kitchen table she pushed a chair to the side of the refrigerator and stood on it to reach the corn flakes and a banana from the top of the fridge. She repeated this motion to grab a bowl from the shelf. Using a butter knife, because she couldn't use a steak knife, Gardena carefully made small slices of banana's to place in her mother's cereal. After pouring the milk over the flakes and fruit she was proud of her creation. "This is beautiful", she thought. She wished she had a serving tray and a rose to give to her mother to make the breakfast even more special.

    Cautiously, Gardena took small steps carrying the breakfast bowl into the living room where her mother slept. She kneeled down towards her mother, nudged her gently and spoke in the softest tone possible.

    "Ma, I made you breakfast." Her mother turned on her side and raised her head. She was still sleepy. She made a partial smile at Gardena, patted her head and said, "Thank you, baby." Lynn looked at Gardena

CHAPTER 2 LONGING

and took the bowl. She wasn't hungry but tried to eat from the breakfast that was made for her anyway. She loved Gardena, not in the same way that she loved her sons. Gardena had always been close to her. She remembered when she first brought Gardena home and her parents picked up from Hutzel hospital. Her mother instinctively told her how, "She had to do right by this child." Lynn took offense to that. With all of her heart, she thought she was doing right by all of her children. Every decision she made was for her children. She had to become a whore in order to pay rent where her first son's father stayed. She continued to walk the streets and find new Johns in order to feed the second son growing inside of her. She needed to get sober in order to take care of the daughter she now had. But losing the addiction to one drug, made Lynn dependent on another and she wanted so badly to stop drinking, but it called to her. Most days she was unable to function without it. And as she looked into Gardena's eyes, this small beautiful child that accepted and loved her for who she was, she felt guilty for placing her second to her drink. But as she thought about trying to go sober she realized it would be a battle she would have to fight at another time.

She sat up and spooned her cereal dodging the bananas in the bowl. She ate three spoonfuls before getting up from the floor and made her way into the kitchen. She sat the bowl on the kitchen table and headed for the cabinets to get her daily dose of medicine. She grabbed the fifth of Po Pov, nearly empty and took the last two swallows. She held the bottle up to the light, tilted as if she had missed some of the drink and then held it upside down to her lips again. Then she tossed the bottle in the trash.

"Mama?", Gardena tugged at her mother's shirt tail. "Are you done?" She held the bowl up to her mother to see.

"Yeah baby." Gardena left the kitchen to pour the unfinished cereal into the toilet. Her mother began to look through the kitchen drawers hoping to find enough change for her next drink. Gardena returned to the kitchen, not disturbing her mother and began to wash the dishes that had been left the night before.

"Mama, can I go over to Tracey's and show her the dolls you and Uncle Thomas bought me?"

"After you wash up and brush your teeth." Gardena placed the dishes she washed into the plastic dish rack to the right of the counter and then she ran into the bathroom, slamming the door behind her. "Don't slam my doors!" Her mother shouted from the kitchen table as she lit a cigarette.

Gardena stood at the bathroom sink and ran the hot water on a wash cloth. She washed her face, under her arms, her private area and in between her toes, while singing "Double Dutch Bus", which was her favorite song this week. She tried to remember all of the words to the song, but could only recite the chorus. She picked up her toothbrush and placed a dime size amount of toothpaste on it and brushed her teeth. Then she turned off the faucet, and reached for the door knob with a towel wrapped loosely around her body. She swung the door open with so much force that it slammed into the bathroom wall.

"Don't be tearing up my house!" Her mother yelled from the kitchen.

"Sorry." Gardena yelled back as she quickly tip toed to her bedroom. There she grabbed a pair of under ware, her plaid shorts and a green tank top from her dresser. She forced her feet into a pair of pink jellied sandals.

Gardena loved the summer. She would sit in her classroom, during the late days of May and the early days of June, at Custard Elementary, counting down the days, a month in advance for summer vacation. The days in school leading up to the three months off seemed like an eternity to Gardena. Day in and day out, before the final days of vacation, were filled with the same routine. The teacher would read books aloud to the students in the morning. They would complete their arithmetic first, their spelling second and their grammar last. Then they would have lunch in the school's gym that doubled as a lunchroom, and only then would they be allowed recess.

Unlike the other children, who complained that it

was too hot to go outside, Gardena didn't mind the hot sun baking her skin or bleaching her sandy brown hair. She would play double dutch with some of the older girls or swing on the monkey bars with the boys and even play tag with some of the children who also enjoyed their fifteen minutes of freedom. But the time was not nearly enough for Gardena and more of the teacher's readings awaited her back in the classroom. In the afternoon, the teachers were told to keep the lights off or down to the use of only one as to cool the un-air conditioned rooms. Gardena took this time to nap, as God blew his cool breath through the open windows. "Thirty more days. Twenty more days. Ten more days." Until finally, there was only one more day until school ended. She would count each day left to herself right before dosing off until summer vacation became a reality.

Gardena raced through the house and out the front door carrying a baby doll in each hand, hoping that Tracey could come out to play. She had neglected to put lotion on her arms and legs like her mother had told her to do so many times before, but the early summer air beckoned her and she couldn't wait to bathe in the tolerable heat.

As soon as Gardena lifted her eyes to view Tracey's porch, she could see that Tracey was already seated on the steps playing jax. Tracey was two years older than Gardena. She was tall for her age and thin

CHAPTER 2   LONGING

with beautiful clear chocolate skin. Her hair was jet black and it wasn't much longer than Gardena's, but her grandmother kept her hair neat with two thick French braids on the left and right sides of her head. Her big bright eyes, teeth and dimples melted Gardena's heart whenever she saw them and Gardena hoped they would be friends for life.

Tracey lived with her father and his mother. She didn't know where her mother was or if she was still alive. Tracey did know that her mother had a drinking problem and when she drank she would tell her horrible things. More than once she had told Tracey she wished she were never born or how she hated being her mother. Gardena felt sad for Tracey, but proud that her mother would never treat her the way Tracey's mother did.

One evening, Tracey's mother came home from being out all night and began cursing and screaming at her. Tracey had stayed up the night her mother was missing, crying because her father couldn't find her mother and Tracey feared the worse. She had called Gardena on the phone and told her about her mother being missing and the feelings she felt, before Gardena's mother told her to hang up the phone.

The screams, on the evening of Tracey's mother's return, turned into slaps and they came crashing down on Tracey's face, forcing her to plummet to the ground and causing her lip to bleed. Gardena was on her own front porch that evening when she saw what happened to Tracey. Instead of playing at Tracey's house, Gardena's mother insisted that she stay home and for Tracey to come to their house and play sometimes. Witnessing the terrible fate of her best friend, Gardena raced into the house, verbalizing what she had seen to her mother. She was surprised at her mother's response. She didn't go outside to help Tracey. She walked to the front door, closed it and told Gardena to mind her own business.

"That's their business. You don't know what that girl did. I know bet not nobody ever find out my business either or what goes on in my house or I'm gonna beat you so bad it'll kill you! Now you stay yo' little ass in the house."

Gardena's head lowered. She didn't contest what her mother had said or done. She walked slowly over to the couch that was positioned in front of their large picture window, thinking about the words her mother had just said. The words stuck with Gardena as she sat on the couch, watching Tracey take her beating. "Maybe Tracey told a family secret?" She thought. "Maybe she's being beat because Tracey told that her mother drank and said mean things to her?" Gardena sat there watching unable to break away from the window when Tracey's grandmother came outside to help her. But the woman was too strong for the elderly woman and Tracey's mother pushed her to the

CHAPTER 2 LONGING

ground. When she tired of beating Tracey, she went into the house. The old woman picked herself off of the ground and tried her best to help Tracey. Moments later Tracey's father pulled up in his brown Thunderbird. He got out of his car, helped Tracey to her feet and then they all went into the house. Gardena left the window and retreated to her room and that was the last time Gardena saw Tracey's mother.

"Tracey?" Gardena called from across the street. "Look at what I got!" Gardena darted across the street, forgetting to look both ways for cars. She was so excited about the new baby dolls she had gotten from K-Mart. The dolls were twins, one in pink, the other in blue and Gardena swung them by their arms as she reached Tracey's porch.

"Look!" She stated as she held the dolls up in the air and close to Tracey's face.

"Oh, these are pretty black babies." Tracey always made comments about black and white to Gardena and everyone else for that matter. Her father and the Mosque they attended on Wyoming and Puritan had taught her about white people and slavery. Tracey's family was Muslim and although Gardena wasn't certain what it meant to be Muslim, other than they read from a book called the Koran, they didn't eat pork and they went to church a lot, she did understand they had a dislike for white people.

When Tracey would have sleepovers, her father, Reuben, would sometimes tell them stories from his past. He was a dark skinned tall man. At one point in his life he was thin, but the belly protruding over his belt told his age more than his face now. Gardena knew he had to be at least forty years old because his hair had started turning gray around the edges. He was handsome, not a wrinkle or mark on his face, which was surprising to Gardena after all he had experienced. Gardena would look at him and wonder about her own father. Many times she asked her mother about her dad. In the beginning, her mother would tell her stories that he was in the army or had to go into hiding from the mob. All of these lies never satisfied Gardena's want to know her dad and she continued to ask her mother more questions about him, until finally one day her mother told her she didn't know who her daddy was and to stop asking her about him. Not knowing who her father was crushed Gardena's heart. And the more she would watch the love, affection and attention Reuben showed Tracey, the more she longed for her own father.

Reuben would sit in his olive colored Lazy Boy recliner and tell how he got out of going to the Vietnam War because he lost both of his index fingers in an accident at the plant where he worked. He joked about it saying, "Those presses came down right on time, 'cause I had got my draft letter in the mail that day!" Tracey would smile and comment about how she still loved him even though he only had eight fingers and he would tell her he loved her back.

"But I did almost lose my life a couple of times though." Tracey's father would continue. "Did I ever tell ya'll about when I went to Alabama to help out with the voter registration drive?" The girls would shake their heads no, although they heard him tell the story many times. "Well," he began. "It was me and a whole lotta other college students going down to Birmingham to set the whites right and make sure the blacks had the right to vote if they wanted to. It was 1961 and we was just pulling up at the bus depot in Birmingham when all these white folks just started attacking the bus. I mean they was hittin' the bus with rocks, bats and they had clubs and all types of shit waiting to beat the crap outta us. See back then, in the south, black people couldn't vote. And if you tried to they made you take these stupid ass tests that you couldn't pass or you could lose yo' job or maybe even yo' life!" The girls looked shocked and stunned as Reuben's eye widened with his statement. "Yeah, those crackers were crazy! Anyway, them white men start coming on the bus, pulling us off the bus, beatin' us on the way out the door. I mean we left there with our faces swollen, noses bloody, brains hanging out our heads. They taught us some positions to protect ourselves from the beatings, because they knew like we did, that the beatings were sure to come, but when yo' arm feels the heat and the pain from bein' clubbed with a bat, hell ain't nothing a protective position can do for you." He excused himself for a moment and disappeared into his bedroom. Tracey talked about her father and Gardena could tell she was proud of him. She wished she knew her father too, this way she could share with Tracey some of the heroic things he had done. Reuben returned to his seat, coughing and smelling like burnt skunk, but continuing with his stories.

"Now, I didn't know about them cats, but I couldn't take that shit for long. So as soon as we got back, I got on my schooling and that was the last they saw of me. Hell, wouldn't gonna lose my life. No sir. Now, that don't make me no coward. I just knew there were other ways to get the job done. See while Martin L. King and those others, SNCC and SCLC were talking that don't fight back crap, I was thinking why the hell not!" Gardena struggled to think what the letters Reuben had said stood for. "Shit, not me. I wanted to hit the first cracker back that hit me with a bat. And that's what Malcolm X taught! But we couldn't do that so I left. I finished as much schooling as I was gonna do, met some people, worked a little and came back home looking for me a steady job. Now I bet ya'll didn't know this, but Detroit is one racists ass city!" Again Gardena struggled with the

CHAPTER 2 LONGING

vocabulary. "Do ya'll know we still have problems moving into neighborhoods where there is a lotta whites? I mean damn! It's 1977 and we still can't live where we wanna? Now I know a lot of them crackers then moved and all, but some of 'em, they still here trying to keep us down." Tracey responded in agreement. "That's right, my baby know the truth, 'cause I teach her!" Tracey, proud to be her father's protégé, smiled as he gave her a high five. "When I came back, Mayor Cavanaugh had lost his damn mind. That cracker created some type of gang squad, S.T.R.E.S.S., that only ganged up on black people! Now my baby knows I'm from the streets, all that education ain't changed none of that. So I'm hitting the clubs, hangin' out with pushers and hookers too, and somebody told me this trick I knew got popped in the back while running away from them bastards! She was running away. How could you do that? I don't care what the woman did for a living, right is right and wrong is damn wrong." He took a moment to collect his thoughts. "Anyway a few years later it was a big riot over there on 12th street near Clairmont. Fire everywhere. The police raided a party for some vets I knew. I was gonna go, but mama was sick, so I stayed with her. Glad I didn't go, hell I would have been all caught up in that shit. People, white and black, was lootin' stores and stealin' shit. I asked my man Jay to get me a T.V. That motherfucka had the nerve to tell me he'd sell me one. That was the last time I gave his ass some free smoke. Anyway, somehow, my name was brought up in this shit and they wanna charge me with theft. So I left and went to Chicago. And from what I done told ya'll, ya'll should know, if there is something going on like a protest or conflict that some black people is involved in I'm there. So through acquaintances I get hooked up with the Chicago chapter of the Black Panther Party. Oooo we! They were some out cold cats. They didn't care about shit but their own and wouldn't no police with guns gonna stop 'em 'cause they had guns too! We actually helped people. Fed kids, took care of the elderly, shit, I even remember the ten point plan," he looked at the ceiling as though the words were plastered above him. "We want freedom, we want employment, we want decent housing, we want health care, um..," he struggled to remember the rest. "Well I remembered some of 'em. We was some bad cats. I enjoyed every moment I spent with those brothers. But they was hot! Not only were the police all over 'em, but so was the FBI and once Hoover put yo' ass on a list, it was pretty much over for you. Huey went to jail on trumped up charges. Seal was sent to jail and those motherfuckas violated his civil rights. Little Bobby was killed. Fred was killed. It was just too many people dying and going to jail and I knew I had to get back home. So I did. These S.O.B.'s here had dropped those fake ass charges against me by then so I got a job in the plant. Then I met Tracey's mother and not too long after my beautiful Nubian princess was born." With that he kissed Tracey on the forehead and patted Gardena on the head. She wished he were her father. "Good night girls. I don't want to bore ya'll with all my tales. I'm tired. I'm going to bed now." And he left the room.

The girls sat outside on Tracey's porch for hours playing with the dolls. They would pretend that they each had a child and they would visit one another at the other's home. They changed the dolls clothing, switching it with the other's and even made diapers for the dolls out of newspapers that Tracey had retrieved from inside of her house. Their play was interrupted when Tracey's grandmother announced she had to get ready for Mosque. Gardena wanted to go with them, but her mother had forbidden it before. Her mother stated, "Jesus is the only God in my house!" and Gardena never asked again.

Gardena ran across the street, back to her house, holding her dolls close to her chest. She opened the screen door and threw her dolls down on the living room sofa. She could hear her mother in the kitchen scrambling through the drawers and cabinets looking for something. She took off her sandals and left them by the door, and took a seat on the couch. Her mother came into the living room telling her to take her shoes and dolls to her room. Gardena did as she was told.

As she entered the living room again, she saw her mother lifting the couch cushions.

"What you looking for Mama? Ma?"

"Forty-five more cents." Her mother spoke anxiously aloud not hearing the question asked of her.

"Gardena, you got some money in yo' piggy bank?"

"Yes Mama."

"How much?"

"I don't know."

"Can you guess?"

"Yeah."

"Then how much?"

"I don't know. Some quarters, dimes and I think a dollar or two."

"Okay." Gardena's mother walked towards the back of the house and entered Gardena's room. Gardena followed her mother and saw her counting the money that was in her bank.

"Mama, that's my money."

"I know, but mama needs a couple of dollars."

"For what?"

"That's none of your damn business. You wouldn't have it if I didn't give it to you." Her mother snapped at Gardena quickly, turned and continued to count the money. With a sadden face and tears swelling in her eyes, Gardena walked over slowly and gently touched her mother's arm.

CHAPTER 2 LONGING

"But I was saving it to buy you a present." The touch on her mother's arm startled her and as a reflex she slapped Gardena to the floor. The child was struck with such force that she hit the floor twice before hitting the back of her head against a used dresser in the room. Gardena's mother continued to thumb through the change and dollar bills before realizing that the whimpering sound she heard was coming from Gardena. She stuffed the money into her pocket, taking all of it except a few pennies. She then turned to Gardena.

"Oh baby I'm sorry. Mama thought you were trying to fight with me or something. You did grab my arm pretty hard." She kneeled down to Gardena. "Look, I'm gonna go to the corner store and I'll be right back. I'll even pick you up some penny candy and a Faygo, okay?" She helped Gardena off the floor, patted her head and headed towards the door. She didn't look back at Gardena when she left out of the house, instead she yelled, "Be back in a little while!" and closed the door behind her.

Gardena stood there, still, unable to move. The only movement from her was the tears running down her cheeks. "I was a bad girl." She thought. "Mama's not going to the store; she's going to leave me." Panic rose from the depths of her insides as her mind began to ponder the thoughts of her mother never coming back. "What am I going to do? How can I get her to come back? Why didn't I just leave her alone when she took the money?" Her eyes raced around the room as if searching the walls, the ceiling and the floor for answers. "What if something happens to her like Tracey's mom?" And then without notice, a burst of pain shot from her loins, raced through her throat and from her mouth and she screamed. She dropped to the floor yelling at the top of her lungs, "I hate myself! I hate myself! I'm so stupid! Please mama don't leave me! Come back mama! I promise I'll be good! I'll get better!" She cried uncontrollably. "I'll get better! Just please don't leave! Mama please don't go!" She screamed, "I'm sorry Mama! I'm so sorry! Please!" Gardena dropped to her knees and began punching the floor, then her legs, pleading continuously for her mother to come back.

Her agony could be heard echoing throughout the empty rooms of the house. The pain she inflicted on her legs couldn't measure up to the pain running through her body. She was alone. She was hurt and her love for mama grew deeper as she prayed for God to send her mother home with forgiveness in her heart. The tears and crying and prayers turned into tired sleepiness and Gardena curled into a ball on the floor and fell asleep.

Darkness crept into the house like a spider seeking shelter in stealth. And the awkward silence of the house called to Gardena in dreams bringing back

CHAPTER 2   LONGING

memories of the love her mother once had for her.

* * * * * * * *

It was Labor Day and Gardena, her two brothers, her mother and a new uncle went to Belle Isle Island. It was quite a long drive from their home to the island but Gardena didn't mind. Her new uncle drove a Lincoln Continental with a sunroof and he allowed Gardena to stand up through the ceiling of his car during the drive. Once they reached Jefferson Avenue, Gardena watched the strange but interesting people walking the avenue as they drove by. Girls in short shorts with tube tops waving and laughing at boys. Elderly men and women jogged down the street in a group for exercise and the liquor stores were full of men and women standing outside of the doors laughing and arguing. As they stopped at a red light, a 1967 light blue convertible Cadillac Fleetwood pulled along side of them. An older man drove the car with a younger woman on the passenger side. He was wearing a Dobbs hat, slightly tilted and she let her hair hang long, flowing in the wind. "Flashlight" played loudly on his stereo and Gardena began to sing along with the song, *"Ooo, I just can't find the beat"*. Her mother turned around in her seat to smile at Gardena, who smiled back, bouncing to the bass ringing from the car next to them. Her brothers sat uninterested. The light turned green and the Cadillac sped off, Gardena's uncle turned right onto the bridge that led to Belle Isle. Gardena loved looking over into the Detroit River that looked clean and refreshing. She stood up, peeking her body through the sunroof hoping to catch the midst of the river from the blowing wind on her face. The welcome clock positioned at the end of the bridge was beautifully decorated with white and red flowers and they circled the large park until they found the perfect place to park.

    The island was beautiful in late summer with glistening water and multiple colors of vegetation. They were having a bar-b-que. Her mother brought Faygo pops, ribs, hot dogs and chips. Her mother was stunning. She wore a short skirt and tank top blouse. Her tall slender figure did not give in to curves, but Gardena thought she could be a model nonetheless. D-Man and Kory, Gardena's brothers brought a ball to throw and they ran over by the swings to play with it. Gardena, took her time admiring how wonderful she looked in her new summer dress her mother bought. The flowers in her dress matched the scenery of wild flowers in the tall-uncut grass of the island, and she took small steps trying to catch butterflies as they landed on the open blossoms. The wind brought refreshing cool breezes from the river and she held her arms wide opened and lifted her face to the heavens as to thank God for this magnificent day. Her family was with her. This is what life and living meant. The strength of existence was made possible through strong family bonds for Gardena and she wanted nothing more but for this day to continue forever. She laid in the grass counting how many bees would fly by not noticing her still body. It was fascinating for her to see the bee come close to her as it pollinated the flowers beside her. The bee didn't frighten Gardena. It could not hurt her with its string. Her mother, her brothers, and uncle would save her from that. Instead she saw the bee much like herself, searching for ways to keep everyday just like this one. As she followed it with her eyes from flower to flower, she thought that it too wanted the strength that only family could bring. The bee much like Gardena could face anything, with family and she smiled. The courage that came from family was enough strength to face any enemy even one as small as a bee.

"Gardena?" Her mother called to her in a sweet peaceful voice. Gardena sat up from the grass and looked to her mother who was motioning for her to come to her. Slowly she stood and then skipped towards the boys who were now putting ketchup and mustard on their hot dogs. She quickened her pace, running through the tall grassy weeds allowing them to whip her body and face as she moved up to the picnic table.

"Hot dog please!" She said smiling as her new uncle put a hot one from the grill on the bun and handed it to her. "Thank you." She replied as she slowly took a bite, juggling the meat around in her opened mouth to cool it down before she swallowed. As she sat there eating her hot dog and drinking her pop she watched her mother laugh, hug and kiss the man she called uncle. Gardena thought it odd for her mother to be kissing her uncle. Weren't they both brother and sister? She moved toward her brothers to ask what was going on.

"Kory, why is mama kissing uncle on the mouth like that?" She asked puzzled by the events but innocent to reality.

"Dummy!" Kory snapped at Gardena. "That ain't our real uncle."

"Naw, he ain't." D-Man added. "That's ma's boyfriend. She always calls 'em uncle to us. Like we don't know" Gardena seemed confused. Her brothers had to be lying because her mother would never lie to her.

"Maybe he is like an uncle from a long time ago and they just friendly to each other now." Gardena came to the immediate defense of her mother.

"You just stupid, you believe anything she tells you. She ain't nothing but a liar and a drunk." D-Man shouted at Gardena, angry at her inability to see what was really happening.

"Naw, you a lie! You just mad with mama. You always be talking about mama like you hate her. You and Kory jealous 'cause she loves me more than ya'll and she keeps me at home with her." Gardena had said it. What if they told mama what she said? That would make mama angry. Mama always told her never to tell the boys she loved her best. She didn't want her boys to feel bad. She didn't want them to know that all she really wanted was Gardena and she wished she never had them. But Gardena said it. She told the secret she was to keep between her and her mother. The secret only a mother and daughter could share. Now it was out and Gardena was to blame. Hesitantly Gardena tried to fix the mistake by denying her mother said such things. She told her brothers that she made it all up.

"Wouldn't care if you or her said it." Kory replied.

"Far as I'm concerned she ain't my mother, Grandma is."

D-Man looked at Gardena and said, "Just wait she gone get rid of you too. Just wait and see. The only reason you still around is because you keep kissing her ass!"

Gardena's mouth fell wide open. She held her mouth open so long her jaw felt as though it had locked. The boys went off toward the shore of the Detroit River and began skipping rocks across the water. She couldn't move. She could feel the breeze of the wind with the chill of the water, she could hear the bees buzzing by, but she could no longer participate in the serenity of nature. Her courage was gone. She only imagined what if the boys were right. Could her mother really discard her like an empty bottle of vodka? The feelings of her uncertainty intensified as she heard the laughter and smelled the liquor from her mother and uncle linger through the air.

* * * * * * * *

The laughter Gardena heard in her dream began to resonate through the walls of her bedroom, and slowly she opened her eyes. She lifted her head off of the floor and saw the light from the living room peek into the darkness of her room. The laughter she heard was real. She thanked God for bringing her mama home. Gardena eased out of her bedroom slowly, entering the hallway like a timid swimmer into the ocean from the sandy shore. Tears were still flowing from her eyes and she sniffled all the way to the front of the house. "Ma?" She asked quietly, fearing to disturb her mother. She remembered how upset she had become the last time Gardena interfered with her pleasures.

"Gardena, baby come here." Her mother was laughing while sitting on the floor between the legs of another white male stranger. "This is Gardena, baby. And this is your new uncle, Simon." Simon smiled but didn't speak, nor did he reach out his hand for hers. He just smiled and leaned back on the sofa, still rubbing on her mother's shoulders.

CHAPTER 2 LONGING

"Hi Uncle Simon." Gardena replied, uncertain what to make of this new uncle. She could only think of what her brothers had said about her mother being a liar. They called mama a slut, tramp and a whore. They told her, mama was sleeping around with all kinds of men and deep down Gardena knew what they said was true. But the question why still lingered in Gardena. Gardena didn't understand the need her mother had to be with all of these strange men.

"Go fix some Cheerios, girl and watch TV." Her mother said before she and her new uncle began to kiss.

Not wanting to upset her mother, Gardena left the living room without hesitation. She made the cereal and went to her room. The thirteen-inch television only got channel 50 and "The Facts of Life" was almost at the end of its program. Tootie was Gardena's favorite character on the show. She always wore her roller skates and never fell once. Gardena asked Santa one Christmas for a pair, but mama said Santa was low on money. Gardena wanted to ask why Santa needed money when the elves made all of the toys, but the tone of her mother's voice was firm and unwilling to tolerate questioning from a child, so Gardena went without.

Chapter 3

STRANGER IN THE HOUSE

Two years had gone by and Gardena's brothers visited her mother's home less frequently. Gardena didn't mind this. This only meant that she would have more alone time with her mother, except uncle Simon was living with them now. The weekend parties of lust and sin ended as Simon didn't want to be bothered with mama's drunk friends. So the air changed in the house.

The sweet smell of happiness was gradually replaced with sour sorrow. The color in the house also differed than before. The bright walls of semi gloss white were now eggshell dingy to sight. The curtains were never drawn to allow sunlight in and smoke filled the overcrowding bungalow. Even when

Gardena looked at the house from the outside while she played, it looked stranger than the other homes on the street.

It was early one morning when Gardena first heard the slap that sent her mother twirling into the dresser and pounding on flesh mixed with the sound of her mother's cries. She wanted to leave her room and help her mother, but she was too frightened to move. So she sat up in her bed crying. Gardena was confused and scared. Inside her heart raced and she panicked fleeing to the safety under her bed as she heard more of her mother's screams, as she ran past her door. Gardena tried to drown out the horror by covering her ears, but it didn't work. Then her mother's body came flying into Gardena's room and onto the floor next to Gardena's bed.

"Bitch! I said you do as I say!" Simon said as his fists crashed into Gardena's mother's face. Blood from her mother's lip managed to splatter on Gardena's face. "You hear me bitch? I'll kill your black ass! Bitch!" Simon's fist made contact with Gardena's mother three more times before he left her bleeding on Gardena's floor.

Slowly Gardena crawled from her hiding space and touched her mother on the chest. The shriek of pain from her mother forced her to jump back in fear. She sat on her knees crying, telling her mother she was sorry for not helping her. She said she was sorry for not jumping in and taking the blows for her. But most of all, she was sorry she couldn't take the pain away. Carefully Gardena's mother picked herself off of the floor and walked hunched over to the door, holding her ribs. She didn't notice Gardena or acknowledge anything that was said. Instead, she turned the doorknob, left the room and headed down the hallway toward the kitchen. Gardena followed behind her, but not too closely. She was still crying softly wondering what her mother was thinking. But as she stood in the hallway watching her mother in the kitchen shuffle through the cabinets, she knew the only thing on her mind was a drink. The fifth of Po Pov was half full and her mother turned the bottle up to her lips. Gardena thought she was drinking forever, but in reality her mother only guzzled down a little of the drink before setting it down on the counter.

"Do you want me to make you something to eat?" Gardena inquired as her mother took a seat at the kitchen table, clutching on to her drink. After staring blindly at Gardena for a moment, she took another swallow from the bottle and replied.

"No baby. I'll make you something. Let me go to the bathroom first." Gardena's mother carefully rose from her seat and went into the hallway and disappeared at the right turn. Gardena sat silently and waited for her mother's return.

In the bathroom, her mother stood at the sink and

lifted her head to the mirror. Her face and right eye were swollen and blood trickled from the lump protruding from the left side of her lips. She ran a washcloth under cool water and carefully patted them. She paused a moment, beginning to cry and threw the cloth down on the sink. "Why?" was all she could mutter. Then she cupped her hands under the running water and splashed it on her face. Again she looked in the mirror at the aging the drinking and beatings had caused on her appearance. She wanted it to end. But how could she stop the drinking without something else to replace it? How could she leave Simon with nowhere to go and no job to earn enough money for herself and her daughter? She felt hopeless inside. This is not the life she meant to live when she started anew. She was supposed to live happily ever after, she and Gardena, in a beautiful home with a magnificent garden. Instead, her dream was now a nightmare and she had no way of waking up from it. She opened the medicine cabinet and took out a small compact of foundation. Slowly she applied the make-up to her face, trying to hide the damage Simon left behind. She then took her lipstick, eyeliner and mascara and did her best to look fresh and appealing to the world.

Gardena's mother reappeared in the kitchen, a few minutes later, with a clean face. Smiling she said, "So what you want baby? Pancakes and bacon?" Gardena began to smile, kicked her feet under the table and her

CHAPTER 3   STRANGER IN THE HOUSE   65

body bounced with joy. She loved her mother's pancakes. They were always light, fluffy and buttery. Gardena's mother took two skillets from the cabinet and the pancake mix. She then grabbed the bacon and butter from the fridge. She carefully cut the butter from the block and turned on the fire under the skillet. The smell of the bacon sizzling on the stove replaced the sour scent in the house. As she moved around the kitchen, she smiled at Gardena and patted her head. This pleased Gardena so. It seemed to Gardena that once again she was safe and her mother's love had returned to the full luster of when they first moved into their home. They sat and ate their breakfast together, laughing and talking and Gardena knew this was the most perfect relationship that a daughter and mother could share.

Gardena helped her mother clear the table and wash the dishes. Gardena was proud to help her mother; it made her feel like a big girl and she thought of herself as a little mama. As they continued with their joyful chore, Simon walked into the kitchen.

"Didn't make me anything? What's wrong with my girls? You want me to starve to death or something?" He said while picking his fingers and leaning against the door opening.

"Oh, I'm sorry, baby. Gardena was hungry and so I, I ..."

"It's okay." Simon said cutting her off. "I have to

go out anyway. I'll just pick up something while I'm out." He walked over to Gardena's mother and kissed her on the cheek, then patted Gardena's head and walked out of the kitchen side door. Gardena didn't know what to make of his actions. She was confused. Just earlier Simon was enraged, beating on her mother. Why did he kiss her now? Why was he so calm and peaceful? Why did he look at her with love in his eyes? The questions were mounting in her mind and while her mother continued to talk and laugh, Gardena couldn't help but ask a question about Simon's behavior.

"Ma? Why is Uncle Simon being so nice now?" Her question forced an uncomfortable silence into the room.

"Gardena, why can't you just be glad that he is?" Her mother's happy tone now changed. It was more firm and edging toward being irritated.

"I just was wondering..."

"Listen," her mother cut her off. "I don't know, but I'm just glad he is. Let him kick yo' ass some and see if you'll be wanting to know why!" She poured the dishwater out of the extremely large plastic bowl they used to wash dishes in, threw the dish towel into the sink and left the kitchen.

Gardena stood alone, wondering. She didn't know how she upset her mother or why she said what she did. All Gardena knew is that she changed a

CHAPTER 3 STRANGER IN THE HOUSE

meaningful joyous occasion with her mother into one of frustration and anger. Again, it was Gardena's fault everything was wrong and she failed yet again to be a good daughter to her mother.

The day grew into night and Gardena sat in her room playing with her dolls her mother got from Goodwill for Christmas. She remembered the day as if it were yesterday.

* * * * * * * *

The days of believing in Santa were over for Gardena, so she begged her mother to take her to Goodwill for a few toys to open on Christmas day. When her mother agreed, she was delighted and ran to put on her coat and gloves.

Together they walked to the bus stop. It was cold and waiting on the DDOT seemed as though it took forever, but Gardena didn't mind. She was with her mother and would have presents this year on Christmas day, making it one of the best years in a long time. Gardena's mother reached into her coat pocket and pulled out a pint of vodka. She took a long swallow, closed it up and returned it to her hiding place. She saw Gardena staring and began to explain. "It's to help keep me warm." Gardena thought it was all right as her mother's winter coat was thin, old and worn.

The bus dropped them off at a church on Puritan and Livernois, which served as a distribution center for the less fortunate. They stood in a long line out front that slowly moved them toward the front door. With every step forward, Gardena's mother took another sip of her drink, until finally they reached the front of the line and the drink was gone.

"How many kids?" the white man sitting behind a school desk asked. Gardena's mother looked puzzled and confused.

"Three. Two boys and me." Gardena replied with their ages, as her mother's intoxication prevented her from answering. They were sent down the hall with a slip of paper to give to a man at the counter. He instructed others to collect toys for one girl, age 7 and two boys, ages 11 and 9. The toys were packed in a huge Goodwill bag and Gardena and her mother were sent on their way.

While waiting for the bus to pick them up from their stop, Gardena noticed her mother moving squirmishly, dancing around in a panic. "What's wrong mama?" Gardena asked while holding on tightly to her bag of toys.

"Girl, mama got to pee! Stay here." Her mother ran into the Church's Chicken that stood behind the bus stop. A few minutes later she came back out of the restaurant relieved to have released the pressure on her bladder. She had also bought a two-piece chicken snack to share with Gardena. Gardena was just as pleased that her mother made it to a restroom in order to avoid an unsightly embarrassment. The bus picked them up shortly after they finished their snack and Gardena's mother paid their fares. As it was crowded, they took the first available seats on the bus, which happened to be on opposite sides of each other. As the bus drove on, they made funny faces at one another. They laughed when people noticed what they were doing. Then the bus stopped and picked up more passengers. A group of teenagers and Tracey entered the bus. Instinctively, Gardena tried to hide the large bold Goodwill print on the big bag of toys by covering it with her small hand. Unsuccessful, she stared at the floor hoping to become invisible.

"Hey Gardena!" Tracey said as she smiled and walked to the back of the bus with the teenaged girls. Although Gardena knew Tracey did not celebrate Christmas she thought Tracey would have said something about her having to accept handouts. But she didn't. Gardena felt as though God must have hidden the words on the bag from Tracey, because she walked by without saying a word. Gardena whispered a "thank you" to Him for not allowing her friend to notice or mention the toys for less fortunate children.

* * * * * * *

Gardena sat smiling from the pleasant memory when the loud force of the front door slamming ended her play. She knew Simon was home as he called to her mother from the front room. She could hear her mother's footsteps walking past her door swiftly into the living room. They talked, quietly at first. But soon the voices rose as hard and loud as thunder. And without notice, Mother Nature cracked her whip into the sky. The sky split and the bright flash of lightening followed. Another crack crashed into the home and screams rang out from unsuspecting witnesses. Her fury was terrible, unrelenting and unmerciful. Again and again, the cracking sound reminded Gardena of a bad thunderstorm. But outside, the skies were clear and the earth remained calm and dry. Mother was the only person experiencing the storm, but Gardena was the one wet with tears.

Chapter 4

TRAPPED

Gardena's brother Kory decided to come over to their mother's house for the weekend and he immediately disliked Simon. Kory also resented that his mother insisted that he call Simon daddy. He decided to stay outside from the early morning hours until the late evening, when he could come in, eat dinner and go to bed. He could see, from the look of their mother that Simon had been beating her. When he questioned Gardena, she would tell him stories of how their mother fell or that she bumped into something. These were lies Gardena learned to tell as she heard her mother telling them to their neighbors. But the bumps into walls and falling over chair legs did not settle well with the Kory. Her black eye, swollen lips and sprang wrist told the story of her abuse.

"Gardena? Why you be lying so much. You know he beating mama." Kory said as he tied his gym shoe.

"No. He don't be hitting mama. She did fall. I seen it."

"Look, you can lie all you want to. But he gonna start hitting you too, then what you gonna do? I'm gonna tell grandma." Kory stated as he was now dribbling a basketball.

"Don't do that! Then she gonna put mama in jail."Gardena replied in fear of losing her mother.

"What?" Kory said angered by his sister. "Why would grandma do that?"

"I heard her tell mama one night on the phone. She said she would tell the police on her."

Kory began to walk down the street. "I'm just glad I don't live here." He said, and then he left.

Gardena played on her porch alone because Tracey was at Mosque. She took out of her book bag her Disney coloring book that her mother had picked up for her from a party store when she purchased her liquor and a small pack of crayons. She sat and colored Snow White first. She colored her black because she thought Tracey would like it. And then she thought to herself that all of the characters should be black as well. While sitting and coloring in her book, she heard loud cursing and confusion down the street. At first she didn't pay any attention to the noise and

CHAPTER 4 TRAPPED

continued her activity. But as the sounds grew louder, she stood up. Unable to see what was happening, she walked two doors down and saw that her brother was in a fight.

Simon and Gardena's mother were sitting on the front couch watching "Welcome Back Carter" on his floor model television, when Gardena ran into the house frantically. "What's the matter girl?" her mother asked as she sat up from the couch.

"Kory in a fight." The child said breathing heavily.

"Lynn, I told you about those damn boys. The last time D-Man got into a fight. They're nothing but trouble!" Simon yelled at Gardena's mother, put his Budweiser can on the cocktail table and headed outside. Moments later he returned, "Take his ass over to your mother's, before I kick the shit out of him and you."

"Okay baby."

"Why I got to go mama? Why don't you just get rid of his fat white ass?" Kory said with anger and hatred in his voice while tears flowed from his eyes.

"You piece of shit!" Simon responded as his hand slapped Kory across the face.

Gardena screamed and her mother rushed to Kory's side trying to pick him up from the floor and move him out of the door before he experienced the full wrath of Simon. "What's wrong with you boy? You don't talk to yo' daddy like that!"

"He ain't my daddy!"

"And I wouldn't want to be, you black bastard! Get him out of here Lynn before I beat your black ass!"

"I'm leavin'. Come on Gardena."

"No, she'll stay here with me. This way, I know you're coming back."

Kory and his mother left the house. Gardena ran to the window, listened as her mother started the car and watched them pull out of the driveway. She couldn't believe her mother had left her alone with Simon.

Gardena stayed at the window, staring a long time before Simon called her to take a bath. He never made a bath for her before, but she knew she took one around 8 o'clock every night. Her mother had been gone for a half hour and although Gardena was unsure of the distance from her home to her grandmother's, she thought tonight it would be okay for her to take a later bath. "Can I wait 'til mama gets back?"

"No. Come on, take the bath and get it over with." Simon spoke with a peaceful and gentle tone.

"Now Gardena!" The bass in his voice made Gardena leave the window and head toward the bathroom.

She felt very uncomfortable entering the bathroom with Simon, but he didn't stay longer than to check the temperature of the water. He closed the door behind him after telling Gardena to be careful and not to leave the bar of soap in the tub. Gardena felt safe as she locked the door behind him and began to undress. She knew her mother should be home soon to tuck her in and kiss her before she fell asleep.

Gardena sat in the tub allowing the soap to escape from her hands before grabbing it and a washcloth to begin cleaning her body. Although she was only nine, Gardena's breast had already begun to swell and her hips were full. She was a little girl in a young adolescent body. She stood and ran the cloth gently across her arms and breasts and tried to reach her back. She then moved the cloth to her legs, thighs and on to her feet and in between her toes. She stood carefully washing between her legs as not to rub too hard making herself burn from the soap later. As with most kids, Gardena loved splashing around in the water, pretending to swim. When Simon yelled for her to stop, she could hear he was on the phone. She hoped he was talking with her mother and she was coming home soon to put her to bed.

Gardena exited the tub, wrapping an old towel around her mature body. As she opened the door, she jumped, startled at the sight of Simon who was standing at the door. "Your mother said she won't be home tonight. She had to take Kory to the hospital for stitches. Now you go to bed." Simon turned and walked away crushing a beer can in his hand on his way back into the living room.

Gardena felt alone and abandoned. Simon hit Kory so hard he needed medical attention and her mother left her alone in the house with this monster. Gardena did what Simon said. She went to her room, closed the door and put on her nightgown. She slipped into the bed covers pulling them tightly under her chin, and she closed her eyes thinking about her mother and why she didn't come home. All of the thoughts from years ago built up into tears that ran from her eyes. Her mother finally left her alone, alone with a strange man she was forced to call daddy, although he made it clear to her he was not her father.

The dark shadows on the wall, made by the moonlight, haunted her. They teased her and danced in celebration of her abandonment. And she squeezed her eyes hard to block the images and held her breath to fight back the tears. "Mama, where are you? Did you forget about me? Was I really like the thrown away bottle of vodka? Mama please come home. Come home tonight!" This was all she could think about, until finally peace came by way of dreams.

* * * * * * *

The rain was falling hard and Gardena stared out of the window, watching. Each raindrop reminded her of the days that had come and gone with nothing substantial enough to remember them by. Her days, they too fell like raindrops, one by one, ending in an oblivion of nothingness. So she sat, hoping the rain

CHAPTER 4 TRAPPED 77

would end singing, "Rain, rain, go away. Come back another day." But it poured even heavier. Then, without notice, a lonely white dog caught her eyes. He sniffed around as though he was looking for something to eat and although the water from the heavens poured down without mercy, the animal's hunger was more important than shelter.

Gardena couldn't help but open the front door and run to his aid. The dog immediately ran toward the porch and into Gardena's welcoming arms. He licked her cheeks, her lips and chin in gratitude of her opening herself to him. She brought the dog into the house, rubbing and stroking her hands over his coarse fur. In return, the dog licked her more. She hadn't asked her mother or Simon if keeping the dog would be okay; instead she took the dog into the kitchen, opened the refrigerator and fed him lunchmeat and hot dogs. The hungry dog gobbled down the cold cuts in a few bites, wagging his tail and begging for more.

"You must be really hungry." Gardena smiled at the dog as she fed him more lunch meat from the package. With the bite of one hot dog, the dog's teeth had caught her finger and she began to bleed. The pain wrenched through her body and she began to cry. But he noticed Gardena's pain and walked toward her and began licking her face to soothe her. Happy to see that he cared for her feelings she opened up to him even more, giving him more treats. Again the dog bit her finger and the blood ran even more profusely, than the time before and with more pain. Gardena screamed and thought to run to her mother to free her from this beast and take the pain away, but he had her cornered and continued to bite at her, breathing heavily and growling. She told him to stop. To get away from her, but he lunged toward her biting her many more times, barking loudly, paralyzing her movements. She squirmed around, trying to find a way of escaping his reach, but there was no way out. The panic and horror of what he was doing to her made her body go numb. She was trapped, there was no way out and her mother was not coming to save her. She sat there and allowed him to bite at her, lick her and pound up against her body for what seemed like hours to Gardena. Then without notice, he stopped. Simon looked at her with gentle eyes and released a white mucus on her clothes.

Chapter 5

ALONE

Gardena's mother returned in the morning and Simon had already left for work. Gardena could hear her mother call to her, but she was too afraid to answer. She covered her head with the sheet, hoping to disappear. She was ashamed of what happened to her last night and didn't want her mother to see her face. Inside, Gardena thought her mother would know what Simon had done to her by her look and her smell. She was afraid that if her mother found out she might get angry with her for allowing it to happen. Worst of all, she feared her mother leaving her for good with the dog that stole her innocence.

"Gardena? Where you at baby?" Her mother hurried to her room, opened the door and pulled back the covers from her head. "Why you hiding, baby? Are you mad with Mama?" Gardena shook her head, no. "Good then. Get up so I can make you some pancakes." Her mother left gleefully and went into the kitchen. Gardena could hear her rattling the pots and pans to find the right one for the pancakes and bacon. Slowly she got out of the bed, her thighs ached and were moist, the nipples on her breasts sore. She moved into the bathroom and closed the door behind her. She took a washcloth from the sink and ran warm water over it. She began to spread her legs and wash delicately between them. The soreness caused her to pause, but she continued to wipe. She brought the towel up to the sink to rinse it and was shocked to see blood on the rag. She wanted desperately to tell her mother and beg her mother to take her to the hospital, but instead she rinsed the towel, wiped her private area again, turned off the water, pulled up her panties and left the bathroom. She could hear her mother yell to her to hurry into the kitchen to eat, and she replied that she would. She walked into her room, closed the door and put on a clean pair of panties, a blouse and shorts.

    Gardena then walked into the kitchen and sat at the table with her mother. Picking up the fork, her mother smiled, patted her head and said, "Girl you better eat up!" as she placed a whole strip of bacon into her mouth. "Simon must of had to be at work

CHAPTER 5 ALONE

early. He don't never leave this early in the morning. Hell it's only 7 o'clock." She smiled at Gardena and shoved the pancakes on her fork into her mouth. "You want some orange juice?" Gardena nodded yes and her mother got up from the table, removed the carton from the fridge and poured it into a glass from the dish rack. "So, you and Simon was okay alone last night?"

The thought of being alone with Simon made Gardena shutter and she was afraid to answer the question her mother inquired of her. Gardena was certain if she told her mother what had happened she would be upset with her. On the other hand, if she lied and told her mother everything was fine, her mother would see right through her and confront Simon. Confronting Simon only meant more abuse, pain and hatred, and this hatred would be directed toward Gardena.

"Gardena?" She jumped in her seat fearing the intense frustration in her mother's voice. "Girl damn, did you hear me? How was you and Simon when I left last night?"

"Okay, I guess..."

"You guess?"

"Yeah mama, I just missed you a lot."

"Oh that's sweet." Gardena's mother took her seat again at the table. "Did you obey him? You know good little girls listen to their daddies."

"Yes mama. I did what he told me to." The thought of her mother calling him her daddy and what he had done to her made her stomach turn. As Gardena sat fighting back the bile rising in her throat, she could hear her mother continuously talking about Simon being her father and how much he loved and cared for them until the vomit rose into her mouth, jerking her body and forcing her to flee to the bathroom.

"Baby, you okay?" Her mother said following behind her.

"I just don't feel good mama."

Her mother touched her forehead and handed her tissue to wipe her mouth, "You don't feel like you got a fever. Maybe you just got a stomach virus. You go lie down. Mama will take care of you."

Gardena left the bathroom and went back into her room. Her mother made her put on her pajamas and take a nap. "I'll bring you some soup later." She put a bucket by the bed, in case Gardena had another emergency, she wouldn't have to leave the bed. "I love you baby." And with that she left the room.

Gardena laid in the bed, pondering on the events that took place. Why would Simon do what he had done to her? How could he do that to her mother? The thoughts began to make her sick again so she tried to push them out of her mind. But the harder she tried, the more powerful the images of him on top of her,

CHAPTER 5 ALONE

inside of her became. She leaned over the bed and struggled to keep the vomit from getting on her bed covers. "Ma?" She called to her mother, hoping she would come quickly to clean the mess she had just made and to make her feel better. "Ma!" Gardena yelled louder, but there was still no response. So Gardena made her way out of the bed, creeping slowly to avoid more pain in her legs. When she reached the living room, her mother was passed out on the couch, sleeping and drunk. She clung to the empty bottle of vodka, like a child would a doll. Gardena walked over to her and whispered, "Mama?", but it only caused her to stir. Not wanting to disturb her, because she had been up all night with Kory at the hospital, she left her side and went back to her room.

Gardena sat up in her bed contemplating what Simon had done to her. She wanted to tell someone. She needed to tell someone to help her deal with the pain she was feeling inside. She decided to go outside, while her mother slept and talk to Tracey. Tracey was her best friend and although her mother warned her about telling outsiders what went on in her house, she thought Tracey would keep her secret.

She grabbed some clothes from her dresser and quickly dressed. Then she left her room, and took the bucket to the bathroom and quietly walked past her mother and opened the door. Before leaving her porch, she took a deep breath and headed across the street.

She rang the doorbell and when Tracey's grandmother answered the door, she asked if Tracey could come out to play. Tracey appeared moments later with sidewalk chalk in her hands.

"Wanna play hopscotch?" Tracey smiled and immediately Gardena felt warm inside.

"Sure. I'll help draw." The girls took the chalk into the driveway and began to draw the rectangles and squares for their game. Although Gardena was sore, she helped Tracey search for a couple of white landscaping rocks from Tracey's grandmother's flower bed and they began the game.

The girls played for hours, alternating between hopscotch, jax and jump rope, until finally they were tired enough to take a break and have a cup of pink lemon Kool-Aid and chocolate chip cookies Tracey's grandmother had brought out to them.

"Tracey?" Gardena began to ask her a question.

"Yeah?"

"Never mind."

"Naw. What? Tell me?"

"Okay, but you can't tell nobody." Gardena said as she placed her cookie on her lap.

"Okay, I promise."

"First, you tell me. You ever had sex before?"

Tracey's face showed her amazement of what Gardena was about to tell her.

"Naw! Ugh! That's nasty girl. Why? You did?"

CHAPTER 5 ALONE

Gardena's head lowered in shame.

"No. I just wanted to know if you did. I mean you are older than me."

"Well, I did play with it."

"Play with what?"

"My coochie." Tracey's smile widened and Gardena's eyes grew big.

"Did it hurt?"

"No. Why would it?"

"You didn't put nothing in it?"

"In my coochie? Naw girl!"

"Well, I had something in my coochie last night." Gardena spoke softly.

"Really? What?"

"I don't wanna say."

"Girl come on. I ain't gonna tell nobody. What did you put in there?"

Gardena's head lowered once again and she spoke even more softly than she did before. "I didn't put nothing in it. Simon did." For a moment there was silence between them. And Gardena did not lift her eyes to look Tracey in the face.

"Simon put his thing in you?" Tracey said with such concern. "Ain't he yo' mama's boyfriend?"

Gardena just nodded her head, yes. Then she began to cry. She tried to verbalize to Tracey what happened the night before, but most of her words were inaudible from her sobs. Tracey sat and hugged

Gardena tight. She said she was sorry that Simon raped her and her mother wasn't there to help. Tracey told Gardena that her father could stop Simon from ever doing that to her again, but Gardena refused the help for fear of her mother's beating that would kill her for telling the family's business.

Gardena wiped her eyes and the streetlights started to blink, a signal they were about to come on, and she knew she had to go home. Before she left Tracey she reminded her of her promise and walked away.

Later that evening, there was a knock on the door as Simon sat on the couch watching television and Gardena's mother washed the dinner dishes. Reuben was standing in front of the door and Simon invited him in.

"Where's Gardena?" He demanded.

"Excuse me? Who in the hell do you think you are coming to my house this late at night asking for my daughter?" Simon responded.

"She ain't yo' daughter cracker!" He pushed past Simon and came into the house. Simon fell backward onto the arm of the couch.

"Lynn, where's Gardena?"

Reuben yelled throughout the house as Gardena's mother appeared from the kitchen and Gardena came running from her bedroom. Simon followed Reuben as he moved into the hallway of their home, cursing words behind him. Reuben didn't flinch. He only said a few words to Simon as he continued down the hallway.

"This cracker touch you baby?" He said as he met Gardena in the hall. Gardena looked shocked and confused.

"Touched her? What the hell you talking 'bout Reuben? And you just can't be walking up in my house like this." Gardena's mother spoke with a kitchen towel in her hand.

"This girl told my baby that this cracker stuck his penis in her!"

Gardena's mother's mouth flew open. Simon stopped talking and everyone stared at Gardena.

"Now don't be afraid baby. Did he or didn't he put his thing inside yo' body?" Reuben insisted on an answer. Gardena's heart dropped into her stomach. Tracey told. Now she had to decide to tell the truth and risk being beat to death by her mother or losing her mother by being taken away from their home. She was confused and she was alone.

"Well, girl did he?" He turned around to look at Simon. "'Cause if he did I'll crack his head wide open right now."

"What? You won't do anything but get your black ass out of my house." He reached for Reuben who grabbed him and quickly twisted his arm behind his back pinning him to the wall.

"Stop it Reuben or I'm gonna call the police!" Gardena's mother shouted.

"Good, call the damn police. That way when this baby says that cracker put is dick up in her his ass will go to jail. How could you let this happen Lynn? This white man," he pushed Simon harder against the wall, "mean that much to you that you would let him take yo' black princess's innocence? Rape her of her youth? This the kind of shit that happens when you fuck around with a cracker! Now tell us girl, I promise he will *not* hurt you. Did he do it?"

Gardena remembered the last promise she made with Tracey. Tracey promised she wouldn't tell her father about what Simon had done to her, but she did. If Gardena said that Simon did violate her, Reuben couldn't convince her that his promise to make him pay for what he had done would actually happen. So Gardena told him it was not true. She told Reuben that she had made up the entire story of Simon touching her. Reuben released Simon from his hold, promised that if he heard of it again he would send the police himself and then he left.

Simon looked at Gardena, mumbled she was nothing but trouble like her brothers, entered the kitchen to get a beer and went back to his seat on the couch. Gardena and her mother stood in the hallway together. She instructed Gardena to go into the bedroom and wait for her. When her mother appeared in the bedroom she had her favorite leather belt, she called Black Beauty and that she used to whip the children with. It was the same belt she had for years. She beat Gardena for two hours, only taking breaks to catch her breath. Gardena thought she was going to die. Simon could hear Gardena's screams and crying enter the living room. He grinned.

Chapter 6

DEMONS ARE REAL

It had been days since Simon touched Gardena and everything appeared to be normal again. She was on punishment for telling Tracey what happened and couldn't go outside, but since she was no longer allowed to play with Tracey she didn't mind staying in the house. Kory and D-Man stopped coming over and her mother drank her spirits as though they were fresh springs from Canadian mountains. Sometimes everything seemed loving, but Gardena knew appearances were deceiving. During the day, the sun kept away the violent devil in Simon that preyed on her mother. The demon grew inside of Simon, controlling him as soon as the sun would set, and freed him as the sun rose. At times, Gardena could hear Simon beating her mother from midnight until he had to get ready for work the next day, breaking only to catch his breath, get a beer or have a smoke. He took so much pleasure in causing her mother physical pain. Often Simon would push her through Gardena's door and while punching her in the face, look up at Gardena and smile. He frightened her. She knew no person could be capable of such brutality.

She heard her brothers say their grandmother talked of spirits, demons and the devil, and how they could take over the human body and make them do things to hurt themselves or others. A few years ago her mother had taken her to see the film "The Exorcist" and she thought that Simon too would be able to turn his head in a 360-degree circle without breaking his neck. Or maybe, he would levitate off of the bed. Gardena was certain she wanted to call a priest, the police or someone, but without a telephone, and no one she could run to without telling her family secrets, she kept it locked inside and prayed to God herself.

One morning, her mother insisted on taking her to school to discuss her failing grades with the teacher. For the first time in her life, Gardena was embarrassed to be seen with her mother. The drinking consumed her and as soon as the liquor touched her lips she was practically incapable of doing anything other than passing out. Her mother looked older than her years

CHAPTER 6 DEMONS ARE REAL

and she smelled of strong cigarettes and urine. She stumbled when she walked, often times falling down. Her hair fell out and she wore an old matted short wig to cover the balding spots on her head. The make-up was useless on the black eyes and bruises Simon left behind. And she would choose to buy liquor over clothes.

Gardena pleaded with her mother to write a note to the teacher, but her mother refused and walked her to school. She had already begun drinking and Gardena could see from her stumbling she was drunk. She tried to walk ahead of her mother, but her mother constantly called to her to slow down. In the building, as the children were putting their books into their lockers, they would stop, stare and point at Gardena's mother. She tried her best to turn the right corner and enter the main office before the other children noticed her, but the children had seen her mother slip and fall and laughter filled the hall as Gardena rushed to her side to help her up.

In the office, her mother spoke loudly and aggressive to the office manager demanding to see the teacher who was failing her baby. Gardena, already sunken in her seat, sank further down on the bench. When the woman behind the counter finally called the teacher to the office, they were allowed to go into the conference room to talk.

"Why you failing my baby?" Gardena's mother

demanded.

"Well, Ms. Williams, Gardena's grades have been slipping for sometime now. I tried to call but your phone is disconnected. I sent letters to your home, but I didn't hear from you." The teacher replied in a calm professional manner.

"What letters? I ain't got no damn mail from ya'll."

Gardena sat with her chin in her chest listening to her mother's slurring speech. "Gardena? You been messin' wit my mail?"

She shook her head, no.

"I can assure you Ms. Williams, I sent the letters."

"Well why cain't my baby pass?"

"I'm afraid it's the end of the school year. She's already missed so many assignments in class not to mention the homework. I've tried talking to her about it, but she says something about a demon is preventing her from doing her work."

"A demon? Oh hell naw!"

"That's what she told me. I tried to get a better understanding of what she meant, but she won't talk to me. It's almost as though she's hiding something."

"She ain't hidin' shit! This little motherfucka gonna get her ass beat if she don't start actin' like she got some damn sense."

"Well all of that isn't necessary. Have you tried your social worker? Maybe asking family services for

CHAPTER 6   DEMONS ARE REAL

some assistance or a referral to have her to talk with someone?"

"I don't need nobody to talk to her! This here is my daughter! I'm the only one know what to do. So you saying she gotta make dis grade up? Uh?"

"Yes, I'm afraid she does. She hasn't grasped the concepts needed to pass third grade and I don't feel confident about sending her to the fourth. I'm sorry."

"That's okay. But I'll take care of this shit at home."

Gardena's mother insisted on taking her home, so she collected her things and headed out the office with her mother. She wished the teacher hadn't mentioned anything about the demon in her home and she was certain she would get a whipping for telling. On the eight block walk home, Gardena listened to her mother curse and yell at her for telling the teacher something "as stupid as a demon in their house" and using it as an excuse not to do school work. She continued by saying, "She wasn't raising dummies in her house and if she wanted to be a dumb ass she could hit the streets".

As they arrived home, she instructed Gardena to go to her room, take off her pants and wait for her. Gardena knew she had to guzzle down her energy drink and find Black Beauty. She appeared in Gardena's room moments later and swung the belt high over her shoulder and down on Gardena's bare skin. She did this several times before leaving the room with, "Now your ass better do better in school. Hell you repeating the same grade, so doing the same shit should be easy!" She slammed the door behind her and went back into the kitchen for another drink.

When Simon came home from work, Gardena could hear her mother telling him about her failure. She could hear her explaining to him how she punished her for not doing what was expected. As she sat in her room, Gardena rubbed her welts and wiped her eyes. At that moment she hated her mother. She asked herself how her mother could beat her so easily, when all she ever wanted was to love her mother. She also thought of how her mother could love Simon so freely and he beat her terribly.

"Yes Simon. I love you baby." Gardena could hear her mother say this to Simon just days after he put her eye out. Gardena remembered the event like it was happening before her eyes. "They were drunk." Her conscience spoke aloud in her mind. "Simon was angry. Mama said the wrong thing. Simon slapped her. Mama screamed. 'Why are you screaming now black bitch!' Mama said she didn't mean to. He hit her, and hit her and hit her. Then he saw the Coke bottle and thought the glass would make her see things his way. He hit her with the bottle across the face. She spent six hours in the hospital, got 42 stitches and she loves him." Gardena would never share these

CHAPTER 6   DEMONS ARE REAL

thoughts with anyone. They were her thoughts alone to keep.

Just then Simon stormed into Gardena's room. She jumped in fear of him. "Yes?"

"I need you to go to the basement and put some clothes in the wash."

"But I don't know how and I'm afraid to..."

"Get down there like I said!"

Gardena ran past Simon headed toward the kitchen, which lead to the basement stairs.

Seeing her mother, she stopped to ask if she would go into the basement with her. But her mother told her to do as her father said and not to upset him by asking her to go against his wishes.

Gardena was always afraid of the basement, but she didn't want to make Simon angry, causing him to beat on her mother and mostly giving him reason to beat her. So she went into the dark, damp, and musty basement alone. Not knowing what to do, she sifted through the clothes, trying to mimic the actions of sorting them as her mother would, but it was very hard for her to see with only one swinging light above her head. She worked quickly, putting whites with whites and trying to determine which clothes were considered colored and which were dark. As she sorted through the clothes, she could hear arguing up the stairs. Simon's voice increased and her mother's did as well, but with the strong sound of a slap,

Simon's voice was the last one to be heard. Gardena worked even more frantically to put the washer on the right cycle and place the Tide, Downy and Clorox into the washer until she heard footsteps on the old creaking stairs. She was frightened and her heart pounded hard and fast in her chest. She tried unsuccessfully to focus her eyes on the figure in the dark coming toward her. As it got closer she could see a silhouette of someone or something coming toward her and she prayed it was her mother. But as the person came nearer, under the single swinging light, she could see it was Simon. The fear in her rose to uncontrollable measures. Her mind raced with questions as her fight or flight feelings of anxiety took over her thoughts and her body.

"How are the clothes coming?" Simon stood behind her as she continued to put them into the washing machine.

"Okay. I just had to sort through them like mama do." She moved faster.

"Well, I'm going to keep you company. I know you don't like it down here in the basement, but little ladies should know how to wash clothes. One day when you're a woman you'll have to do it for your husband." Gardena looked at him over her shoulder, he smiled a devilish grin.

"Well that's it for this load. I'm gonna go upstairs."

CHAPTER 6 DEMONS ARE REAL

"I did tell you that you look like a little lady. Didn't I?"

"No." Gardena replied lowering her eyes from his and beginning to walk toward the stairs.

"Where are you going. I'm talking to you."

"I was just gonna go upstairs to help mama."

"Your mama doesn't need your help." He said grabbing her arm and stroking her face.

"But I promised her I would help with dinner."

"No, she'll take care of that. You may look like a woman, but you only need to do one womanly chore and that's the clothes." He moved his hand from her face to her breasts. "You are going to be one fine woman one day. Any man would be happy to have you. I know I am." Simon grabbed Gardena pulling her further away from the stairs into the darkness that the light did not penetrate. He lifted her blouse and fondled her breast. He unbuttoned her pants and began to pull them down.

"Please Simon, don't do this." Gardena tried to free herself from his grasp.

"Shut up you little bitch. Don't be like your mother, a fucking whiner."

"Mama!" Gardena yelled for her mother as she continued to push at Simon and try to break loose of his hold.

"Bitch." Simon slapped her. "You do as I say. That drunk mother of yours can't save you. She does what

I say or she'll be sorry, just like you." And with those words, Simon lifted Gardena up on an old table in the washroom and forced her legs open. She cried when he entered her. She felt sick as he repeated over and over to her "This is my cunt". She continued to call for her mother and Simon didn't stop her, he was too engrossed in what he was doing. Simon took his time filling her up with his manhood, pinching and biting her nipples and breasts. When he was done, he looked at her and said nothing. He just buttoned his pants and headed back upstairs.

Gardena was devastated. Simon had violated her again and this time her mother knew. If her mother wouldn't save her, she thought, then who would? Her mother had traded her for a bottle and fear for her own safety and not the safety of her child. She had betrayed Gardena. Gardena knew then they would never have the kind of mother-daughter relationship that she prayed they would have.

In the dark, Gardena could hear the rain outside hitting the cement by the basement window and she could hear it leaking inside. The sound of the thunder didn't scare her anymore because she was more afraid what awaited her upstairs. So she stayed in the basement and allowed the rainwater to touch her feet. She believed that somehow God's tears would cleanse her body and take Simon's scent away. But the stench of Simon and the mildew smell in the basement told

CHAPTER 6   DEMONS ARE REAL

her she was nasty and she laid down with the rest of the filth and went to sleep.

"Gardena? Gardena? You down there?" Gardena's mother called down the basement stairs in search of her daughter, in the early hours of the morning.

"Mama?"

"Gardena baby, come up stairs."

"No mama. I'm too scared."

"What you got to be scared of girl?"

"Simon. Why didn't you help me mama?"

"Get up here."

Gardena climbed the stairs slowly to keep the pain in her legs at a minimum. "Help you with what?" Her mother said as she reached the top of the stairs.

"Simon."

"You need Simon to help you?"

"No mama," crying, "I needed you to save me from Simon."

"Girl that's nonsense. Simon ain't done nothing to you."

"Yes he did mama. He slapped me and..."

"You probably deserved that. You know yo' mouth getting a little too fast. You should have got yo' ass beat, all that shit you be talkin'." She turned away and moved over to the table where she had already started on a full bottle of Po Pov.

"Mama and he, he,..."

"He what?" The look in her mother's eyes caused

Gardena to hesitate and she said nothing. She knew her mother had to hear what happened. She called out to her mother many times, even after Simon slapped her, but her mother would not come to her aid.

"Now take yo' little ass a shower. Girl you stink! You been sleeping in them dirty clothes. Hell ain't no telling what done crawled on yo' body in that basement. Ha. You might even need to douche, hell it might be something in yo' coochie! Now gone, go."

Gardena left the kitchen, went into the bathroom and ran a shower. She knew inside that her mother heard what Simon was doing to her. After all Simon was very loud with the things he said to Gardena. Her mother just didn't want to believe it, Gardena thought. She would rather believe that Simon was her man, loving and caring, even with his constant beating on her, than to admit he was also a pedophile.

Gardena entered the shower, and began to wash, gently at first, but then she began to scratch her skin. Digging her nails deeper and deeper into her flesh, she believed that she could rid herself of his smell, his dead skin cells, his foul breath and his hair. She scrubbed and tore at her skin so fiercely that she didn't feel the sting of the wounds caused by the shower water. It wasn't until she got out of the shower that she realized how badly she ripped at the skin all over her body. She then carefully dried off and went into her room for a fresh change of clothes.

Chapter 7

ABANDONMENT

Gardena survived another year of being pimped by her mother and sexually abused by Simon. Her mother didn't experience the pain inflicted by Simon as much as she used to. Between the beatings and getting drunk, she would sit and listen to Gardena cry out for her to stop Simon's molestation of her, but to no avail. Her mother would never come to her aid or stop Simon. After a while she stopped screaming for her mother to come. Eventually, Gardena would sit in her bed and wait. She would wait for the darkest hour when he would open her door and she would let him have his way– her face wet her pillow with tears long after Simon finished.

The mother she loved so much finally abandoned

her and she had become an outcast to her brothers. There was nowhere for her to go, no one she could turn to. So Gardena continued to let the devil have her mind, body and soul and entered a place of isolation.

It was morning and Gardena went about her normal routine of getting up from her bed, taking a shower and douching to rid herself of Simon's smell. As she stood in the shower she questioned how these things came to be. Why was she cursed or slated with such bad luck? All she wanted to do is be with her mother, love her mother and have her mother's love in return. But she began to understand this was not to happen.

She turned the knob of the bathroom and wished she entered a different place, but the same sour smell of the house pushed its way into the bathroom as she swung the door inward to leave.

"Guess what baby?" Gardena's mother stated with so much happiness in her voice.

"What Mama?"

"We moving!"

The thought of Gardena and her mother moving seemed like a fantasy. Finally she and her mother would leave Simon behind and try to mend their relationship. With the news of a new house, Gardena had already forgiven her mother. She had forgiven her for drinking, for beating her, for allowing Simon to release his sexual desires on her, but most of all, she

CHAPTER 7   ABONDONMENT

had forgiven her mother for not being perfect and she was willing to start over again.

"We moving?" Gardena replied with relief and a tear in her eye.

"Yeah baby. Simon said this neighborhood is going down 'cause too many black folks renting on this street now. So he bought us a house in the suburbs. Redford girl! What you got to say about that?"

Gardena's face dropped immediately. All hopes of starting anew had been shattered. Simon bought the house. It was Simon's house and she knew moving into a new house with him would mean the same old thing.

"But Mama, why can't you and me just move?"

"Girl I can't afford no place like that!"

"Then why don't Simon move and we stay here?"

"Girl now you sound stupid! What the hell is wrong with you. That man been taking care of you and me. He's a good man."

Gardena wanted so badly to tell her mother what was on her mind. She wanted to tell her that Simon was a devil. That Simon was beating and raping her. That Simon beat the mother she loved. That Simon had even sent away her brothers, her only protection. But mostly, that he had ruined her dream of being with her mother and having the perfect mother daughter relationship. But she understood that telling her mother what she was thinking would definitely mean a slap across the mouth, so she said nothing.

"Oh yeah, yo' brothers coming over to spend the night. Simon said it was okay since they ain't been over in a while. So go clean up your room." Her mother turned to head for the kitchen where she had begun to chop onions for the meal she was preparing. Gardena did as her mother said and went into the bedroom. She began to pick up the few toys she had and placed them in an old box labeled Gardena's toys.

Although the news of moving into a new house with Simon devastated her, she was glad her brothers would be over for the night. She felt safe for the first time in months. She thought to herself there was no way Simon would dare do those things to her with her brothers around. The strength of family rose within her again, but this time it was the security her brothers would bring that made her feel as courageous as a bee.

While cleaning, she could hear the front doorbell ring and the conversation among adults. She could also hear the sounds of children, two boys and she knew D-Man and Kory were there. She rushed the few toys left on the floor into the box and ran to the living room. Her grandparents left before Gardena ran into the living room and into the arms of her brothers who were just as happy to see her. Her mother left them in the living room to finish preparing dinner.

CHAPTER 7 ABONDONMENT

Hugging her brothers and welcoming them back, Gardena noticed how much they had grown. D-Man's was fifteen years old now. His complexion was darker than she had remembered and he was tall and lean. His face handsome and strong with a wide nose and prominent cheek bones and chin. His arms sculpted as he showed off his biceps and his calves were strong and muscular. Kory, who was now thirteen, looked almost the same to her except for his height. His hair was in a short naturally curly afro, his skin a yellow tint with hints of dirt spots around his cheeks and nose. He was almost as tall as D-Man, maybe a few inches shorter than him, but to Gardena they looked like giants towering over her.

"Okay Gardena, dang! What's with all of that." Kory stated lightly pushing her away.

"I'm just happy to see ya'll. So why ya'll over here?"

"Grandma and granddad going to see grandma's mama's in Natchez, so we had to come here 'cause they couldn't take us." D-Man responded angry about the situation.

"Yeah and I bet Simon gonna be trippin' 'cause we over here and he don't like us." Kory added to the conversation.

"So. Who cares about him." Gardena said. "Mama gonna make us pancakes for breakfast and stuff and Simon will be gone to work."

"Mama gonna be drunk!" Kory stated.

Gardena knew he was right and although her instincts rose within her to defend her mother, after years of abuse she couldn't deny the truth any longer.

"D-Man? What you wanna do?" She attempted to change the subject to get her mind off of the dysfunctional family situation she was forced to live in.

"Well, I'm gonna go to sleep." D-Man headed toward Gardena's bedroom.

"Hey," Gardena's mother spoke from the kitchen, entering into the living room. "Ya'll put ya'll things upstairs. That's where ya'll be sleeping."

"But I thought they'd be sleeping in my room with me mama."

"Girl how that look? Two boys sleeping with you."

"But they my brothers."

"I don't care! Simon said that don't look right and that's that. Now boys get yo' stuff and take it up to the attic." The boys picked up their bags without hesitation and started up the stairs. Gardena felt despair and hoped her brothers could hear her cries up in the attic, and be able to rescue her from Simon.

Day grew into evening, and they sat at the kitchen table to eat dinner. Gardena's favorite meal of pork chops, potato salad and string beans sat on the table before her. She said a small pray, hoping that God would answer.

CHAPTER 7 ABONDONMENT

"Dear God;
Please make this a special day. Don't let Mama get drunk. Don't let Simon hit Mama or rape me. Please let this be a good day.
Amen."

And with that she picked up her fork and dove into the potato salad. As they ate, they talked and they laughed. Kory told how he busted his eye by walking on the curb and had to get ten stitches. D-Man told how he beat up a kid on the railroad tracks near his grandmother's home, only to be chased home by the kid's friends and family. They told Gardena and her mother about how the gas was shut off and how they tried to reach their mother unsuccessfully. But because their grandparents had a huge fireplace they camped out in the living room by the fire and it was a fun experience. After they ate, Gardena helped her mother with the dishes and the boys headed to the living room to turn on the television.

The evening gave way to the night and Gardena, her mother and her two brothers sat in the living room watching a Count Scary program. They jumped together at frightening scenes, ate popcorn and laughed at the special effects and make up that looked too fake to be real. They were enjoying themselves when Simon came home drunk.

"Hey, I see the fellas made it here." Simon said as

he stumbled in through the living room door.

"Yeah and I put their things upstairs like you said baby." Gardena's mother quickly jumped off the couch and moved toward Simon to kiss him.

"Well, you little bastards not gonna speak?"

The boys refused to acknowledge his presence and continued to watch their show. Simon was very drunk this night. Although Gardena had seen him drink lots of beer before, she had never known him to slur his words or stumble into things. She knew this would be a night of torment for everyone.

"Well, speak boys. Say hi to your daddy." The boys looked at their mother with hate, and cut their eyes at her. "Don't come over here startin' no shit."

Hesitantly the boys forced a low hi and hello from their mouths. They never turned their eyes from the TV to give Simon the respect Gardena's mother said that men do, by looking a man in the eye. She saw in her brothers the defiance of Simon she could only wish to display. She saw courage in them that she prayed for nightly. Most of all she saw them as protectors who were not afraid of Simon and the wrath he could pour out on them all.

Gardena's comfort was short lived as Simon stumbled over to the couch and grabbed Kory by his collar.

"You little half-breed!" Spit from his mouth sprayed Kory's face as he shouted. "I'll teach you to disrespect me."

D-Man saw the blow coming down on Kory and grabbed Simon's arm. "I'm tired of you pickin' on my brotha!" And with that he used all of his strength to push Simon who went crashing into the cocktail table. The glass in the middle of the table shattered as Simon's tall heavy body fell into it. The shards of glass seemed to ascend into the air in slow motion as Gardena could see fear in Simon's face as she looked at him, her mother, her brothers and then back to Simon. Everything was as though the second hand on the clock had not moved at its normal speed to reach the next tick.

"Motherfucker!" Simon brought Gardena back to reality as he stumbled to pick himself up from the floor. "You black bastards! Wait until I get up."

Gardena scream, "D-Man, Kory go upstairs!"

The boys leaped from the couch, pushing past their mother who was screaming inaudible words and rushing to Simon's aid. Gardena ran with the boys upstairs to the attic after slamming and locking the door behind her. From upstairs they could hear Simon yelling at their mother and him struggling to open the attic door. Then they heard the smashing of more glass, the slap of a hand on skin and the thumps of fists and feet into flesh. Then, silence. Moments later they heard Simon say he was leaving and their mother begging him not to go. The door slammed.

As Gardena and her brothers sat in the attic there was nothing but quiet between them. Gardena sat in a corner, with her knees to her chest, crying without making a sound. She learned to do this from experience. Sometimes the boys would snicker when they heard Simon hitting their mother. Gardena thought she heard D-Man say, "She deserved that," and immediately wanted to tell him how wrong he was. During the beating Simon imposed on her mother, Gardena tightly closed her eyes. She imagined she was the warrior Thor. She would race down the stairs, swing her sacred hammer and slay the demon Simon. She would then look at his dying body and once more with her hammer crush his skull, to end his terrible reign. But she wasn't the Mighty Thor; she was a little girl who locked herself in the attic with her brothers in fear of Simon the Terrible.

Chapter 8

SURRENDER BODY, MIND AND SOUL

The first two days of Simon's absence brought peace into the house. Gardena didn't worry about his nightly rendezvous to her bedroom and her brothers were able to be themselves, causing terror up and down the street. Gardena's mother, however, stayed at the kitchen table, glancing over to the dishes piling up in the sink. Between sips of her drink, and drags of her cigarettes she cried. When she wasn't crying, she yelled and cursed the birth of her sons for driving her man away. Gardena wanted to go to her mother and console her, wipe away her tears, but she was unable to. Her newfound freedom was too much for her to contain. She felt comfortable roaming the house, free of the demon that used to dwell within. She went outside again and sat in the grass pulling up the dandelions that out numbered the grass blades. She played with her dolls as though she was their mother, and her touch was loving and caring as she combed their hair and tucked them in for bed. "This is how a good mother would be." She stared at the dolls, rearranged them and gently kissed their foreheads. "I can't wait to have my babies. I'll never do them like mama did me." This was her vow. She promised herself and future children to be a good mother unlike the mother she had.

In the background of Gardena's play, she could hear the phone ring. The conversation was quick, non-caring and to the point. She thought nothing of it until her mother opened the screen door and called to Kory and D-Man.

She could hear mother telling the boys that their grandparents made it to Lexington, Kentucky and by late night or early morning they should be arriving to pick them up. Gardena didn't mind that Kory and D-Man were leaving; they were a bit too wild and disrespectful to her mother in her opinion. Once they left, she would be alone with her mother and then she would go to her, hold her, kiss her cheek and make things better. Gardena would convince her mother they were better off without Simon and the demons he

CHAPTER 8 SURRENDER BODY, MIND AND SOUL

carried inside. She would say although D-Man and Kory would make their family complete, it was okay if they didn't live with them too.

Gardena smiled and the birds outside of her window sang. They sang of redemption in Gardena's mind–redemption of a relationship between mother and daughter that had gone astray. She thought of how she would help her mother stop drinking by hiding her vodka bottles, replacing the liquor with water or another way. They would take long walks around the neighborhood, because contrary to what Simon said; this was still a good neighborhood to live in. Maybe they could even get a dog, Gardena thought. A German Shepard would protect them from any intruders including Simon if he tried to come back.

Gleefully, Gardena played. She pretended to make dinner for her dolls and set the floor, that she pretended was a table. She spoke in a loving tone to her dolls as she told them to wake up for dinner. "Pork chops, potato salad and string beans was always my favorite dinner when I was a little girl. What is your favorite?" She smiled as she waited for a pretend response. "Well steak is good too Mya. But we don't have that. Tell ya what, the next time I go to the grocery store, I promise to buy you your very own steak. And if you can't eat it all, Mommy will help you because that's what good mothers do for their daughters." As she sat and played for what seemed like hours to Gardena the phone rang again.

The conversation was long, and her mother's voice was sweet, "Sure baby, I miss you. I want you to come back home. My mama called and said they'd be here tonight or early in the morning to get the boys." She paused, "Uh, well she'll be here. She was real excited to hear about the new house you bought. No, she's not gonna go with the boys, she's staying here with us. That's great baby. I'll see you tonight then. You won't have to worry about those bad ass boys, I'm gonna lock them up in the attic" and she made promises that things would be different–different if he came home. She didn't make any demands of him. In her eyes, he could do no wrong. She just wanted him back, and his wishes would be her command.

Her mother hung up the phone after making her pact with the devil. Her daughter's body would be payment for his return and for moving them into a better neighborhood. Inside Gardena's mother felt terrible about her decision. She knew why Simon had asked about Gardena, she wasn't blind to what he had been doing to her. But her inability to put down her drink and her desire to stop him from beating her came at a price. That price was her daughter. She tried to reason with herself by saying, "Gardena will learn a good lesson from this". However, she knew she was only lying to herself. She saw no other alternative, her welfare checks had been cut and the rent was sure to

CHAPTER 8 SURRENDER BODY, MIND AND SOUL

fall behind if Simon wasn't around to pay it. And she thought since she gave Gardena life, the least she could do was keep a roof over their heads.

Gardena knew who was on the other end of the phone without hearing the voice of the caller. Simon. He was coming back and her brothers were leaving tonight. Her mind pondered on whether to tell her brothers what Simon had done to her or not. She remembered vividly the last time she told and she was afraid of what the result would be. But this way, maybe, she too could leave to the safety of her grandparents' home, people she had never met before. But what would her brothers think of her? What would her grandparents think? She thought back to how her brothers talked about the religious nature of her grandmother. Maybe her grandmother would think her to be a sinner, destined for hell, where the fire burned the damned forever and the worms ate your flesh. Or what if her grandfather was like Simon? He too would sneak into her room, fondle her breasts and enter her body. Then there would truly be no place for her to go. Once again, Gardena's options seemed unbearable. So she sat in her room crying, waiting for the return of Simon.

Chapter 9

BETRAYAL

Plates of Hamburger Helper sat on the table before them and Gardena's mother happily told them to dig in. The boys, hungry from play, shoveled spoonfuls of the noodles and meat into their mouths. Gardena sat quiet. She didn't have much of an appetite; instead she separated the noodles from the meat on her plate.

"Girl, better stop playing in your food." Gardena's mother told her while pouring fruit punch Kool-Aid into red plastic cups for the children. "You know it's kids in Africa wish they had something to eat."

Gardena heard her mother, but her body's movements could not catch up with the command that entered her mind.

"So ya'll grandma gonna be here soon. Ya'll ready

to go home?" Gardena's mother asked as she sat back down at the table and picked up her spoon.

"I know I am." D-Man stated while chewing his food.

"Me too." Kory added. "It's getting boring over here. And ain't nobody to play with anymore."

"Well, I don't care about playing with these kids anyway. They always trying to start stuff."

"Yeah. Like that kid down the street." Kory stated before rushing another spoonful of food into his mouth.

"Man that fool was stupid! If he was on Indiana, Ronie would have slaughtered him."

"That's fo' sho! I can see it now. Ronie would've kicked him off his bike, slammed his head on the curb and stomped him. It woulda been over for him, dog." Kory said as he and D-Man stood and gave each other a high five and laughed while taking their seats again.

"Gardena, what's wrong with you?" D-Man asked while scrapping the last of his food onto his spoon. Gardena didn't hear D-Man, nor did she pay any attention to their conversation. She was trapped in a world of her own, a world of torment.

"Gardena. Gardena!" Her mother screamed at her. Gardena shook in her seat. "Did you hear your brother?"

"Yeah." She continued to pick at her food.

"So? You gonna answer him?"

CHAPTER 9 BETRAYAL

"Huh?"

"Are you gonna answer him?"

"Yeah. Nothing. Ain't nothing wrong with me." She glanced up and made eye contact with her mother, and then she looked down at her plate again. Gardena managed to swallow down two spoonfuls of her meal, then she stood from her seat, grabbed her plate and placed it on the counter.

"You done baby?" Her mother asked her as she was leaving the kitchen.

"Yeah." She responded without looking back at her mother. Kory and D-Man said they were finished as well and they left their plates on the table and ran outside.

Although it was evening and the clock on her bedroom wall said it was after 8:00 p.m., the brightness outside gave an afternoon appearance. The sun didn't shine at all that day. The weatherman said it would be partly cloudy. Gardena felt as though the cloud was only over her head; following her around since the phone rang and Simon announced he was returning home.

Gardena didn't play as she sat in her room. She just sat still. She looked down at the dolls she had been playing with and anger began to rise within her. At this moment, she was not afraid of what awaited her, she was angry. She reached down and grabbed one of her dolls from the floor. She then stared at the doll, ripped off its clothes and spanked it.

"You stupid little girl! I wish you were never born! You so stupid! Dumb ass! Good for nothing but a fuck! I hate you! I hate you!" She took a pencil that sat on a makeshift nightstand beside her bed and began stabbing the doll in the face, in the chest and in the pubic area.

Suddenly, Gardena's mother burst into her room. "What in the hell are you doing?" Gardena jumped at the sight of her mother. "What are you doing?" Her mother demanded.

"Nothing."

"The hell you ain't. You poking that doll in the pussy. You some kinda pervert?"

"No mama, I was just..."

"Get yo' ass in my room. I'm gonna teach you to do nasty shit in my house!"

"No mama. I wasn't doing nothing." Gardena began to cry.

"Get yo' ass... now!"

Gardena ran into her mother's room.

"Take down yo' pants."

"Please mama. I won't do it no mo'. Please!"

"I ain't playin' with you!" She grabbed Gardena and wrestled with her to get her pants off. She swung Black Beauty over her shoulder and brought it down with so much force that it cracked into Gardena's skin, instantly leaving a welting mark on her leg. "I..." *crack!*

CHAPTER 9   BETRAYAL

"Done told you..." *crack*! "Not..." *crack*! "to be fuckin' around..." *crack*! "And you..." *crack*! "still actin'..." *crack*! "like you..." *crack*! "ain't..." *crack*! "got no..." *crack*! "you bad..." *crack*! "ass little..." *crack*! "bitch..." *crack*! "don't listen..." *crack*! "to nothing..." *crack*! "nobody say..." *crack*! "better learn to do what you told!" *crack*! *crack*! *crack*! *crack*!

"Yes Mama! Yes!" Gardena screamed, twisted and frantically rub at the stinging marks that were now present all over the lower part of her body, as her mother finished beating her.

"You better be glad I done ran outta breath or I'd beat yo' as some mo'! Now get yo' ass ready to take a bath and when yo' daddy get her you better welcome him back with open arms!"

Gardena ran from her mother's room and into the bathroom, slamming and locking the door behind her.

"You better not slam my damn door no mo' either!" Her mother screamed after her.

Gardena sat on the toilet crying. "Why do she hate me? Why? I love you mama? Why do you hate me?" She sat there asking questions and waiting for an answer from the walls, from the faucets–from God. She got up from the toilet and kneeled down by the tub. She turned on the hot water, neglecting purposely to add the cold water. Under the sink she grabbed the bubbles for the bath and poured in the entire bottle. When the height of the water reached the trap drain,

Gardena turned off the water. She dropped a washcloth in the water before stripping herself of her clothes. She took her right foot and plunged it into the water; unlike she would have done if she were testing the water.

Gardena cringed at the burn of the hot water on her skin, but she took her left foot and plunged it into the water as well. "You're a bad girl. A dirty girl." She told herself trying not to think about the extreme burning around her calves and the heat consuming her feet. She sat in the water; her behind, private area, stomach and back ached from the heat. "You're bad Gardena." She continued to tell herself. And so she sat. She didn't take the bar of soap to cleanse her body, she sat. She didn't lay in the water to allow it cover her breasts, upper back and neck, she sat. She didn't play or pretend to swim, she sat. Gardena sat until the bubbles dissolved and the steaming hot water grew cold.

"Gardena? You didn't drown in there did you girl?" Her mother stood outside the bathroom door.

"No."

"Okay then, hurry up and wash up so you can get out."

"Okay." Gardena stood from the tub, her skin tender, almost raw and wrinkled. She wrapped a towel around her body, opened the bathroom door and headed down toward her room. She could hear

CHAPTER 9 BETRAYAL

that Kory and D-Man had made it in the house and were raiding the refrigerator. In her room, she fumbled through her dresser drawers to find a satin and lace night gown her mother had bought for her from Shopper's World. Simon had told her once that the night gown made her look like a woman, because of the way the lace laid over her breasts. After he had said that she never wore it again. But she would wear it tonight. She thought Simon would like it and maybe even be gentle with her for wearing it.

The shadows of darkness engulfed the last bit of light outside and now it was night. Gardena was unsure if her brothers would be leaving before Simon arrived, but she prayed they would have to be in the home with her until Simon had to go to work. Her mother made the boys go into the attic for the night and Gardena could hear, from her room, her mother turning the key to the pad lock she had installed earlier on the attic door. She knew she was alone.

Her mother had been celebrating Simon's return by cleaning the house, lighting incense and drinking. She bathed which she hadn't done since the morning before he left. She oiled her legs and sprayed perfume in the air before stepping into the descending fragrant moisture. She put on one of her best and most expensive long wigs and waited by the door for Simon.

Gardena sat in her room until she noticed the house was silent. She crept out of her room to get a snack from the fridge. She was very hungry, having not eaten the meal her mother prepared earlier. She craved something to eat. A nice cold apple she thought, a crunchy carrot, or maybe something better, chips! The taste of the salted potatoes made the saliva in her mouth increase and she tiptoed into the kitchen scanning the cabinets and shelves for the Better Made bag she had seen earlier. Her mother laid on the couch, passed out, in a drunken sleep. Gardena knew she was drunk from the half empty pint of Po Pov that sat on the wood in the middle of the destroyed cocktail table. Gardena searched the lower cabinets then the higher cabinets in the kitchen for the chips, but to no avail. "I know I saw those chips. Where is mama hiding 'em?"

She looked on top of the refrigerator, behind the sugar and floor containers on the counter, finally finding the bag in the bread box.

She sat at the table carefully opening the bag as to not make noise and placed a single chip in her mouth. Gardena began to swing her feet under the table in delight of the snack she was eating. The fear of Simon's return left her because she had reasoned if he hadn't come home by now, he probably never would. Engaged in eating, from time to time she would hear her mother stir and she would pause. She didn't want her mother to wake up and become angered with her for not eating all of her dinner, but deciding to eat chips. Instead of taking small bites, she would place

CHAPTER 9 BETRAYAL

the whole chip in her mouth and allow it to melt before chewing.

Without warning, the front door opened and closed. She heard Simon calling to her mother to wake without success. Gardena froze in her seat. She couldn't move, she didn't want to move or Simon would know she was in the kitchen, and he would see the night gown she had chosen for him.

Gardena thought how stupid she must have been for wearing the night gown. She understood that by wearing it, Simon would be even more attracted to her and inside she knew that wasn't what she wanted. She thought to run into her room, but she knew her room provided no safety. She wondered if she could make it to the attic door, unlock it and run upstairs with the boys before Simon could reach her, but she heard his footsteps and knew it was too late to try.

"Hey Gardena. What are you doing up so late?" Simon asked her while reaching into the refrigerator retrieving a beer. Gardena didn't know how to respond. Simon was calm. He hadn't been drinking. Maybe he was different she thought, he didn't notice her night gown. "Gardena?"

"Oh, I was hungry and wanted some chips."

"Does your mother know you're eating them?" Simon asked in a playful manner. Taking a seat at the table beside Gardena. She was unsure what to make of his behavior.

"No. She sleeping."

"Yeah, she is sleeping. She's also drunk. I wish she didn't drink so much. We could be the perfect family almost if she didn't drink." Simon's brow was tight as though set in concentration as though he was trying to think of a solution to the problem. "I know. Maybe together, we could help your mother stop drinking." Surprised at his statement, Gardena wanted to trust him. She thought to herself maybe the demon inside of him was gone. Her brothers told her that demons could be cast out of people by touching their foreheads and saying the name Jesus. Did Simon go to church and let a preacher bind the demon inside him? Why was he so nice to her? It had to be a trap she gathered. He had to want something.

"That's all I been wanting is for mama to stop drinking."

"Well, I know she can't do it alone. So why don't we make a deal? We'll help her stop drinking before we move to our new home. Okay?" Simon added before drinking the last of the beer in his can.

Gardena agreed. He stood from the table, patted Gardena's head, went to the refrigerator and grabbed another beer. "I'll be in the living room watching TV and taking care of your mom if you need me." He left the kitchen.

Gardena thought that Simon may have changed while he was gone. He had never been that nice,

CHAPTER 9   BETRAYAL

loving and caring toward her. She didn't quite know what to make of it. She envisioned in her mind the life she could have with her mother not drinking and Simon not abusing them both. She thought about how they could live together in Redford, he as her father the only father she has ever known, and a beautiful loving mother. One that would walk her to school, play hopscotch with her, and tuck her in at night before bed. These thoughts appealed to Gardena as she began to swing her feet again in enjoyment.

"Gardena? You wanna come in here with me to watch TV and take care of your mother?" Simon called to her from the living room. Thinking nothing of it, she left her chips on the kitchen table and sat on the couch where her mother was lying down. "Don't sit there, you'll disturb your mother and she really needs her rest. Come over here and sit next to me." Simon asked her pleasantly. Gardena was hesitant. "Don't worry. I'm not going to hurt you sweetie." Simon reassured Gardena, who was still leery of his motives.

Cautiously, she walked over to the love seat where Simon sat and took a seat at the opposite end of him. She couldn't make out if he was smiling at her for obeying him, like a child should obey a parent, or if he was staring at her body and the way it looked and moved in the night gown he had made known to her that he liked.

"You wanna watch something scary?" Simon

knew Gardena liked scary movies and "Night of the Living Dead" had just come on. "You should probably sit closer to me. You know how scared you can get." Gardena didn't move. "Okay then suit yourself."

The movie played and Gardena covered her eyes when parts were too scary for her to watch. She jumped and trembled on her area of the love seat.

"Told you. If you ever get too scared down there, I'm right here to protect you." The tone of Simon's voice and the serenity of his actions caused Gardena to let down her guard. She moved closer to him allowing him to wrap his arms around her. "See, now that's better, isn't?"

Momentarily Gardena felt somewhat safe. She hid her face in Simon's chest when she was too afraid to watch a scene. She allowed him to hold her tight when the zombies crashed through windows and knocked down doors. And although this was innocent, Gardena could still see images of Simon on top of her and could feel him inside of her. Simon brushed his hand over her breast and Gardena jumped away from him.

"What's the matter sweetie?" Simon smiled as he pulled her toward him.

"What are you doing?" Fear set in and Gardena's eyes questioned his actions.

"Oh, did I startle you? I'm sorry Gardena. You know I would never try to do anything to hurt you. I

CHAPTER 9 BETRAYAL

only want to make you feel good. Safe." He moved in to kiss her. Gardena rejected him, turning her head towards her mother who was still sleeping on the other couch.

"Sooner or later Gardena you'll realize that your mother gave you to me." Not knowing what to make of what Simon said, Gardena struggled to break free of him. "Do you want to wake your mother? Yeah, maybe she should watch!"

"Watch? Please Simon no don't let mama see you hurt me. Please don't hurt me no more. Please." She began to cry, he wiped the tears from her eyes with his thumbs.

"Your daddy would never hurt you baby. Call me daddy, and I promise I won't hurt you, but you have to be very quiet."

Crying and confused, Gardena tried to mumble the word daddy to Simon. Finally she managed to force it from her throat. "Daddy."

"That's my girl. He pulled her closer to him, hugging her intensely and long. He wrapped Gardena's arms around him and he stroked her hair. The movie played on volume ten in the background and Gardena looked, as far as she could, around the room. When she looked at her mother briefly, she could have sworn her eyes were open, staring at Gardena hugging Simon. But with a blink of Gardena's eyes, her mother's eyes were closed again.

She pulled from Simon.

"Mama?" She spoke softly at first for fear of her mother's anger to see her with Simon. "Mama?" More forcefully she demanded attention from her mother.

"Are you trying to wake her?" Simon yelled and covered Gardena's mouth. "I thought you were gonna be daddy's little girl, but you're disobedient. So you'll just be daddy's little whore!" With that Simon slapped Gardena and she fell back on the couch. He grabbed at her night gown and she fought to keep it down. She constantly screamed for her mother to wake. She called to her brothers to help, but Simon was too strong for her.

"Shut the fuck up!" Simon slapped her again. Gardena did not stop screaming and crying for someone to come to her rescue. Suddenly she could hear banging on the door. The sound came from the attic. Her brothers could hear that something was wrong and they called to whomever to leave their sister alone. They continued to bang and bump up against the door to free themselves and help their sister. Gardena continued to scream as Simon fought with her to lift up her night gown. She looked over at her mother–sleeping. Gardena knew that her mother had to be aware of what Simon was doing to her, but instead chose to do nothing and continue to be in a drunken slumber.

Then, headlights of a car shined through the living

CHAPTER 9 BETRAYAL

room window as though the car was pulling into the driveway. Simon pushed three of his fingers into Gardena's body to make her ready for him. He took one of his fingers, licked it and forced it into Gardena's mouth and told her to suck it. For fear of what he would do to her, she did it and did not bite him. Then he readied himself, suckling her breasts and kissing her neck. Simon loosened his belt buckle and quickly slipped his pants to his knees while still struggling with Gardena. He didn't pay any attention to Gardena's screams or cries, the horn blowing outside, the boys who were still banging on the attic door or Gardena's mother who pretended to be asleep on the couch.

Before he was able to force her legs apart and open them wide enough to move her pelvis closer to his, a loud crash of a bottle silenced Gardena's screams and awoke her mother. D-Man and Kory managed to get out of the attic and D-Man had taken one of their mother's empty vodka bottles and hit Simon over the head. Stunned by the force of the strike, the penetrating glass and the blood rushing down his forehead, Simon fell backward holding his head, almost passing out. Gardena's mother immediately sat up from her sleeping position screaming, "No!" cursing the boys for everything they had done. She rushed to Simon's side trying desperately to hold him as he kept pushing her away and trying not to lose consciousness. Kory had gone over to the door, unlocked it, beckoning to D-Man to get Gardena and hurry outside to their grandparents awaiting them in the car.

Gardena was uncertain what was happening or if it was real. She was finally rescued. Someone had finally cared enough for her to help. The brothers she called liars, when they spoke ill of her mother. The children her mother didn't love. The ones she didn't need or want to live with her, her brothers were her unlikely saviors.

"Come on, hurry up!" Gardena could hear Kory yelling over the cursing of Simon and the screams and cries of her mother. D-Man placed Gardena over his shoulder to carry her outside to the car. She could see her mother crying and Simon bleeding. She could see the home she once lived in and loved left in ruin. She felt the pain of betrayal and the fear of the unknown. As they made their way to the car and opened the door, Gardena's tear filled eyes were blurry and practically visionless. She could hear the voice of an older woman asking her brothers what was wrong and why she was crying, but she couldn't see her face.

On the long ride into the darkness she drifted off to sleep.

Chapter 10

HOPE FOR SOMETHING NEW

Gardena was sleeping when she arrived at her grandparents' home. Her grandfather carried her to the second floor, laying her in the southeast bedroom. He didn't undress her, nor did he kiss her forehead as he pulled the covers up to her chin. He gently patted her head, turned and closed the door behind him.

While in slumber, Gardena dreamed a dream unlike she had before. Instead of dreaming about the abuse she had taken that evening, from her mother and Simon, she peacefully slept and dreamed of a garden. In the garden sat her mother, soiled with dirt from planting flowers; flowers that Gardena couldn't name. They were pink, yellow, white, lavender and orange flowers and the blossoms filled the air with their sweet smells. Her mother was beautiful, wearing a pink and white smock and garden gloves on her hands; her head covered with a rag. She smiled at Gardena, as she ran to and from the porch, being chased by a small white dog. Her feelings were warm and she giggled as the dog barked. Her mother told her to be careful not to run too close to the garden she was planting. But Gardena, being a playful child, managed to get too close to the garden and the dog ran through it. Her mother didn't yell or scream. Instead she told Gardena to come sit beside her. She stroked Gardena's hair and pinched her nose. Gardena could smell the mix of flowers and Chanel perfume her mother wore. Her mother looked into her eyes smiling. The smile showed she was loved, and in return Gardena smiled back. Her mother took her into her arms, hugged and kissed her, then she began to sing:

> *Good morning to you,*
> *Good morning to you,*
> *I'm very happy to see you,*
> *I'm very happy to see you,*
> *Good morning to you!*
> *How do you do?*
> *How do you do?*

CHAPTER 10   HOPE FOR SOMETHING NEW

I'm very happy to see you,
I'm very happy to see you,
Good morning to you.
Good morning to you.
And this is the day that the Lord hath made,
And we shall be glad and REJOICE IN IT!

Gardena, wrapped in the warmth of her mother, slowly began to open her eyes. To her surprise, her mother wasn't the one singing the song to her. Instead there stood an elderly woman, with silver hair, a wrinkled face and a partially gold tooth, smiling down at her.

"Hi baby. You want something to eat? I made bacon and grits." The old woman said. "Now you get outta this bed and come on downstairs with yo' brothers, granddad and me, so you can get something to eat." Then she left the room.

Gardena didn't know what to make of the older woman singing to her as she woke. Who was she? Could she be her grandmother? Why didn't she ask her about what happened? The only thing Gardena could understand was that she missed her mother and it hadn't been a whole day since she last saw her.

FROM THE AUTHOR TO THE READERS

Dear Reader

In today's society, we have a developing need for mothers to reconnect with their daughters. It is easy for us, as a people, to seek out predators who live outside of our households; down the street, around the block or across the nation through Internet connections. However, the predators who live with us, in our homes, often go unnoticed or are rather ignored.

Daughters of mothers who are alcoholics and substance abusers, are more likely to experience many forms of child abuse including being sexually molested by their stepfathers, mother's boyfriends and at times their own biological fathers.

As an educator, I am drawn to the adolescent girl who is displaying unusual characteristics and/or behaviors. Having shared some of the experiences of a relative who was abused, I am cognizant of the possibility that I may have female students who are also being violated. My heart goes out to them and I express my desire to help in any way that I can. Unfortunately, children who are abused rarely talk. Whatever the circumstances may be at home, for them, isolation and denial are their best defense. And it is for this reason I wrote this book.

The goal of this three book series is to open the eyes of the reader, so that they too will become more familiar with the signs and after effects of abuse. The main character, in the first book, is abused at a young age. By the second and third books, we will see how the damaging affects of her abuse shapes her life into adulthood.

As compassionate people, we would love to see Gardena have a happy ending, but only God knows the destiny of an individual. Therefore, you, the reader will have to continue to read to find out.

mother

depressed, I'm thinking she may have been
sitting at the table with only half a candle lit,
taking hard drags from her cigarette
the ashes that carelessly fell off
represented the years of her life
the bright tobacco flared
like the desire to live she once possessed.

as I stood in the darkened doorway,
hands shyly covering my face,
I saw her dying eyes,
her tired hands,
her worried spirit
depressed, she had to have been
sitting, still glassy eyed
the only motion
inhaling of the cigarette and the
cloud of smoke extracting from her lips.

was she thinking of the empty bellies, the darkness
the still coldness in the house?
no, the thoughts had to be deeper than these
her life was in that cigarette

slowly disintegrating before our eyes
her written words, artful expressions
hopes and dreams
inhaled and released from her existence

as I watched her hesitantly put the cigarette out
I knew that was the end of her life
there were no more Salems on the table,
only a dying flame in their place

ABOUT THE AUTHOR

Ucal Finley currently resides in Dearborn, Michigan with her husband and two children. She teaches speech, competitive forensics and drama to high school students for the Detroit Public Schools system.

She completed her undergraduate studies at Marygrove College, in Detroit, earning a Bachelor's of Arts degree in both English and history in 1998. She returned to Marygrove College, in 2000, earning a Master's in Education degree in 2002.

To her credit, Ucal has written three plays, "Blossoming to Freedom", "DePorres Blues" and "'Till Death Do Us Part: The Marriage of Darnell and Darcell", all of which have been produced on a high school level. Her poetry "for him", was the winner of the Amy S. McCombs/ Frederick P. Currier Writing Award. She is also the editor of *Freedom Journey* by Vincent E. Matthews, Jr. Dog in the Garden is her first novel.

Please contact this award winning author at: futurebestsell02@yahoo.com or educ8tor173@comcast.net to:
- Order additional copies of *Dog In The Garden*
- Book Ucal Finley for a speaking engagement
- Offer praise for the book
- Inquire about upcoming book signings, appearances, other special events
- Schedule a book signing
- Arrange for an interview with the author
- Inquire about future projects and works by the author

ADDITIONAL WORKS BY UCAL FINLEY

Blossoming to Freedom

Till Death Do Us Part: The Marriage of Darnell and Darcell

For Him

COMING THIS FALL TO A BOOKSTORE NEAR YOU

DePorres Blues, A Drama in four acts

Book two in the *"Gardena"* Series

Other Literary and Poetic Works

Printed in the United States
63961LVS00002B/53